Jesus, Politics and the Church

Tony Nassif

WinePress Publishing  *Mukilteo, WA 98275*

Contents

Acknowledgment

To my father Elias J. (Tony) Nassif Sr., who has entered the kingdom of God before us. I wish to thank him for having taught so many of us the benefits of hard work and integrity, honor and sensitivity to the needs of the poor and commitment to civic responsibility. God is pleased and we are blessed.

For my mother Adele Nassif who always keeps an open and warm home where all are welcome. Whose hard work with my father provided a strong moral ethic and foundation for life. Always acknowledging God. When growing up I remember her early morning question asking: "Tony, did you say good morning to God and thank Him for waking you up?"

To my beloved grandparents Frank and Mary Ferris whose faith in Jesus Christ was an inspiration to all who knew them. I recall my grandmother who, for no apparent reason, would look at me and say: "Tony, God has been very good to me."

Thanks to my brother Gary, a man greatly gifted by God, who encouraged me to create beyond my own perceived ability. To my sister Alexandria (Sandy), who doesn't know the meaning of the phrase "I can't," pursues the goal no matter what the obstacles. She turns mountains into stepping stones. As well to my brother Don and sister-in-law Denise. Two people through whom God demonstrated his faithfulness when He brought them together. Who can forget my niece Kristen Noel whom God has blessed. She has brought great joy to all of our family.

Last, but certainly not least I wish to thank King Jesus of Nazareth who has given me joy, life and peace.

Tony Nassif

Introduction

In recent years the involvement of Christians in the political process has received a great deal of attention. The concern of many Christians regarding the moral policies of the nation and the social problems it has caused has contributed to this rising tide of Christian activism.

The acceleration of this interest and involvement started with the Moral Majority and then with the Pat Robertson campaign for President in 1988. Presently, this growth has produced such Christian organizations as Concerned Women For America, the Christian Coalition, Family Research Council and many more.

However, there are many who do not believe that Church and State should be mixed. Others believe that the Christian faith is a personal one which should be confined to the four walls of the Church and home. Others believe that it is the Christian responsibility to be active in civic affairs and that the Christian ethic should affect all issues of life.

When the issue of Church involvement in politics began to arise I sought to find out what God thought of the issue. The insights I found were quite remarkable.

In this book I have set out to answer the questions of whether Christians should be involved in politics or not. If they are, to what degree? To what extent are Christians responsible for what happens in society and government? What does the Old Testament teach on this issue? Does the New Testament maintain the same teachings, and in what manner? How did the early Church respond to the civic issues of the day? What, if anything, did the Early Church Fathers have to say about the issue?

These questions are addressed in an understandable and straight forward way—ways that relate to Christians in contemporary America.

In this book I have applied decades of my political experiences. Additionally my diverse experience with Roman Catholic, Eastern Orthodox, Evangelical and Charismatic Churches has also helped give me insight to these questions.

One day as I was sharing my insights with Ralph Reed, the Executive Director of the Christian Coalition, he made a suggestion. He told me., "Write a book Tony." I did and here it is. I pray that it blesses you with a special wisdom and knowledge about your God-given rights as citizens of not only God's Kingdom, but this great nation of ours as well.

Tony Nassif

1

The Beginning of Human Government

To properly understand the role of Christians in human government we need to know its origins and the overall effect it has upon on the civilizations of the world.

The Book of Genesis gives the account of God establishing human government during the creation of the world. It is clear that God systematically created the world and universe in sequential steps.

After the animals were created, God gave Adam authority to name them. In doing so God established the first human government of which Adam was made the head. God's ratification of this authority came when He said:

> *"...and whatsoever Adam called every living creature, that was the name thereof"* Genesis 2:19.

This same principle can be seen in the New Testament when the angel instructed Joseph to name Mary's child

"Jesus." Why wasn't Mary given this message? After all, she was the one chosen to be the Mother of the Lord. Joseph had nothing to do with the incarnation of God in Mary's womb; however, he was to be the virtual caretaker of the "first family of God." He was Jesus' earthly father.

Why do you suppose the naming of Jesus is even considered important? The great Bible teacher and Early Church Father, John Chrysostom answers this question in his homily on the gospel of Matthew 1:21-25, and by association in Luke 2:48. He points out that it was recorded that at the age of twelve, Jesus had found his way back to the temple. When Mary and Joseph went searching for him they found He was in the temple speaking to the doctors of the law. In her chastisement she refers to Joseph as his *father*.

Chrysostom rhetorically questions: Why, since God was Jesus' Father, did Mary call Joseph His father? He answers the question by saying that when the Lord gave Joseph the authority to name the child "Jesus", God put Joseph in the position of the Father's authority. Therefore, Joseph was Jesus' father by positional authority when God gave him the task of naming the Child. Thus, Mary could call Joseph the father of Jesus. (Luke 2:48).

In the same manner when God gave Adam the authority to *name* the animals He established the dominion of Adam over all creation. Thus, we have the first human government established by God through Adam, God's first born being put into the position of supreme authority.

It is important to know that when God established the "government of creation" headed by Adam He was mindful of the future events of today in twentieth century America.

10

He knew that Godly principles would come under attack, and that there would be an issue revolving around Christian involvement in civic affairs. We need to keep in mind that God's actions in time and space are done with three purposes:

First, to affect the desired goal at the point of need. Second, establish a precedent for future generations. Third, to establish an eternal principle revealing more of the desired relationship between God and man.

When God established Adam as the federal head of all Creation, He established the foundation for God's people to be involved in human government.

Consequences of Human Decisions in Human Government

Mankind's authority over creation and human affairs is accompanied by the responsibility and consequences of their actions and decisions. The act of Adam and Eve's rebellion introduced death to creation. Animals die—stars burn out. Plants decay. The whole universe was affected. We can recall the words of the Lord spoken to Adam:

"...cursed is the ground for thy sake; in sorrow shalt thou eat of it all the days of thy life" Genesis 3:17.

Adam's actions affected all within his dominion. It was for this reason that the Lord first went to Adam concerning the problem of their disobedience in eating of the forbidden tree. God was looking for Adam to take responsibility so they could be restored.

Athanasius of Egypt, a fourth century Church Father, rhetorically asks a pointed question in his book, *"On The Incarnation of the Word"*: Since God knew all things why was He asking where Adam was? Why did He not ask where was Eve?

The answer is that Adam was the federal head of creation and God gave him the opportunity to take responsibility for the sin and restore himself and his wife to fellowship with Him. This alone could protect creation from the consequences of rebellion against God which leads to a state of degeneration and death.

Unfortunately, Adam shirked his responsibility by blaming Eve, then by implication blamed God. Consequently, the Lord passed judgment on Adam, Eve, and all creation. Death and decay set in.

Adam and Eve were soon to see the fruit of their rebellion. It brought death to one of their children, Abel—and the curse of God to the other, Cain. Such are the effects of the principle of what I have termed, Subjective Responsibility. This is when the person who is the "head" whether in government or family, makes a decision either turning towards or away from God. The consequences will generally fall on those under their authority.

When God sent the ten plagues on Egypt because Pharaoh would not let Israel go, all the people and land of Egypt suffered.

As I was sharing this with a friend of mine, Jane Boeckmann, she remarked that these people did not have a voice in their government. Yet, they suffered by the actions of Pharoah who disobeyed God. Hearing this makes me feel a greater and more sober responsibility for us who have the ability to have a voice in government. I dare say that the Egyptians would have voted Pharaoh out of office if they had the chance.

As time goes by in the history of Israel we see the Lord confirm this principle through the mouth of Ezekiel when He says:

> *"And I will make the land desolate, because*
> *they have committed a trespass, saith the Lord."*

This same subjective responsibility was also effected on Israel when King David ordered that they should be numbered contrary to the will of God. When the judgment of God came David took responsibility:

> *"...is it not I that commanded the people to be numbered?*
> *Even I it is that have sinned and done this evil deed;*
> *but as for these sheep, what have they done?*
> *Let your hand, I pray thee, O Lord my God, be on*
> *me, and my father's house; but not on thy people*
> *that they should be plagued"* I Chronicles 21:17.

David was the federal head of the nation as was Adam the Federal head of creation. Both sinned and their subjects suffered the consequences.

In the Book of Kings we see Elijah having stopped the rain in Israel for nearly three and a half years. King Ahab tells Elijah that he has brought much trouble to him and Israel. Elijah, on the contrary, says that it was Ahab's wickedness that brought judgment from God. (1 Kings 18:19, 20).

The "Law of Subjective Responsibility"

There is a positive side to what I refer to as the "Law of Subjective Responsibility." One of the greatest of these examples is the testimony of Abraham.

Abraham procured the blessings of God for himself and the children of Israel through his obedience and faith in God. Deuteronomy chapters eight and nine record that the reason the Israelites were being given the promised land was because of God's promise to Abraham.

Thus, we see the blessing passed down through the Law of Subjective Responsibility. It was expressed by God to Abraham in Genesis 22:18 when the Lord promised him that all nations of the earth would be blessed through his "seed."

Abraham acted upon his faith in God's promise. It was then accounted to him as good works which procured the blessing for himself and his future generations. This is evidenced when the Israelites were led out of Egypt by Moses and given the land promised to Abraham. All nations of the earth are blessed through his seed who has now become known as Jesus Christ— the One who took upon Himself the sins of the world.

The Apostle Paul documents this principle in his epistle to the Romans. He writes:

"...for if through the offense of one (Adam) many be dead, much more the grace of God, and the gift...by one man, Jesus Christ, hath abound unto many" Romans 5:15.

Disobedience and rebellion against God will always lead to death. One aspect of "death" can be defined as the decay of society. Corruption in high office, increases the depravity of crime as well as physical death itself. Conversely, obedience to the Lord brings a person into fellowship with the One who is the light of light and the wellspring of life—Jesus Christ our Lord.

When people who ascribe to godly principles of righteousness in their own lives and public policy hold government office, the ensuring effect will be the general peace and prosperity for that nation on a whole.

Has America gone past the point of no return? Definitely not, but the warning signs are quite evident. Natural disasters are more severe and diverse. Crime is more gruesome and the inner cities are deteriorating at a faster rate. However, there is hope for the nation if government leaders act responsibly.

A good example of this can be seen through the eyes of some contemporary high school youth. Then look at the recent statistics on drug abuse as stated in a Reader's Digest article entitled *"Drugs are Back-Big Time,"* by Daniel R. Levine.

Mr. Levine observes that according to the University of Michigan Institute for Social Research drug use among eighth graders has increased 400% since 1992. He observes that during the 1980's drug use actually declined. This is attributed to First Lady Nancy Reagan's "Just Say No" message taking hold on the youth of American Society.

Mrs. Reagan was in the position of exercising social influence on the nation's youth because of the fact that her husband was the President of the United States of America. Through her influence we began seeing the media playing anti-drug use commercials which led to the decline in its' use.

The John Hopkins Children's Center did a study on the effect of these ads. They found that 97% said that the ads convinced them that using drugs was "more dangerous" than previously believed. Seventy one per cent said that the ads discouraged them to use drugs.

This article continues by contrasting the increase in drug use of the 1990's to the decline in anti-drug ads during the same period of time. For example, in 1989, there were 518 drug stories aired on the evening news. By 1994 there were only 78 and that number has been declining since.

In the January 12, 1996 issue of the Daily News newspaper in Los Angeles, a poll by Louis Harris and Associates was quoted as having found, among other information, that 25% (50% in high crime areas) said they do not always feel safe in their own neighborhood.

Nearly one third of those polled said they were fearful of being a victim of drive-by shootings. The percentage increases by nearly 40% among African Americans and Latinos.

In the January 15, 1996 issue of Time Magazine it was pointed out that there is a teenage time bomb of young children growing up in broken homes. Moral leadership is lacking. Strong, positive role models are competing with gangs for the children's attention.

This article points out that there are 30 million children in the U.S. under age ten. While crime is dropping for adults it is soaring for teens. Between 1990 and 1994, the rate for youths between the ages of fourteen and seventeen committing homicides jumped 16%. The rate of homicides committed by adults twenty five and older actually decreased 22%.

In an article in the Los Angeles Times on January 15, 1996 a couple of teenage girls spoke about their experience living in a home without a father. It seems that even in their tender age they see the wisdom of God's plan that a home is to have a mother *and* father. One of the young girls said: *"Without a daddy, all the pressure's on them...that's when all this stuff starts to come in wrong. There's a place for your father and a place for your mother."*

One of the young person's interviewed made an interesting economic and social observation. She said that if her dad were around there would be more money to pay bills, they could save money, and consequently find enough money to get out of the gang infested neighborhood.

Children are searching for stability and society is handing them a broken home for a family and violence as a remedy for problems. It is important that America hears the cry of these children and take the responsibility that God has entrusted to us.

2

God, Government & the American Revolution

The Declaration of Independence, the foundation of our government and society, clearly and articulately states that all mankind is...

> *"...endowed by our creator with certain inalienable rights. Among them is life, liberty and the pursuit of happiness..."*

By this statement the Founding Fathers proclaimed that God the "Creator" gave mankind certain rights. These rights stand above all authority of Monarch, government or institution. When there is a threat to the security of these freedoms it is the duty of God-fearing people to protect and defend them.

The Declaration of Independence marked the birth of our nation when it was signed on July 4, 1776. The signatories stated, in effect, that God gave us our rights and you, King, have infringed upon them. Therefore, we have moral and civil justification to rebel against your tyranny. Thus, we declare our independence from your authority.

Herein we see the root and foundation of the Revolutionary War arising from Biblical truth. This motivated the Founding Father's to throw off the yoke of British tyranny. Samuel Adams, affirmed this when he said: *"Our cause is just...and it was...a Christian duty to defend it."*

John Witherspoon, one of the signatories to the Declaration of Independence, was a member of the Continental Congress for six years. He served on over one hundred Congressional Committees and made the following revolutionary comment: *"True religion and civil liberty is inseparable."*

When the Colonists won their freedom they worked to develop a framework of government for the nation. The primary focus being to protect and secure the enjoyment of those rights given by God.

They labored for extended periods of time without reaching an agreement on how the constitution should be framed. Benjamin Franklin then addressed the delegates. He alluded to the words of Jesus Christ who said that God knows even when one sparrow falls to the ground.(Matthew 10:29) Therefore, he concluded, if a sparrow cannot fall out of the sky without God's knowledge, no kingdom or nation can rise without His help.

He then suggested that a time of prayer be taken to ask for God's help. Shortly thereafter they reconvened the convention and the United States of America had a Constitution. This Constitution established a government which provides for the protected enjoyment of those rights granted by God. Shortly thereafter The Bill of Rights was added. This commenced to establish the specifics of what are those inalienable rights.

In order to properly interpret the Constitution and the Bill of Rights, the will of the Benefactor (God) need be at its heart. To interpret the Constitution without the illumination of the Benefactor's will would be similar to someone buying a Ford vehicle but using a Chrysler owner's manual to understand its' function and operation. It simply will not work. There will be confusion in the operation of the vehicle. Serious damage may also occur to the vehicle and the person attempting to operate it.

The "Owner's Manual" for the Constitution has been the Bible. This has established the standards of ethics and morality. These have been the guiding light of Constitutional interpretation. This set of standards is commonly known as the "Judeo-Christian" ethic. At its heart is the revealed will of the Creator/God through the Bible.

To interpret the Constitution in any other way opens the door to existentialism. Consequently this leads to eliminating moral absolutes which have been the undergirding of this nation for over two hundred years. Such a diversion from our biblical heritage opens the door for abuse and tyranny by extremists from any political perspective.

Those who misinterpret the Constitution refer to the Christian point of view as "extreme right wing." I would take issue with such a description. When the Christian philosophy is viewed through the eyes of truth and sincerity one will see that such a philosophy is neither "right wing" nor "left wing." Rather, it could be well described as common sense, logical and compassionate.

Here are some examples: The Christian philosophy believes that those who have an abundance should give of that abundance to help those who are less fortunate. Not out of coercion but of a willing heart, giving a help *up* and not necessarily a hand *out.*

All the while the Christian philosophy believes that to in debt ones' self to the point of bankruptcy is neither fiscally wise nor morally right. Burdensome debt will lead to bondage.

As I mentioned, the Christian philosophy embodies common sense as well as compassion. One of the best examples of this is the Christian position that sex outside of marriage is wrong.

Nature, science and medicine agree with this position in that sex outside of marriage exposes the participants to disease and possible death through the dreaded A.I.D.S. virus. Science and medicine have concluded that the only "safe sex" is that within marriage between a man and woman. Therefore the time tested position of the Judeo-Christian ethic proves once again to be the common sense, and reasonable position.

Biblical precepts embodied in the Judeo-Christian ethic have always provided the blessings of prosperity and protection for this nation. When we departed from the truths which established this nation, the foundation began degenerating from "solid rock" to "sand." Unless the trend is reversed collapse of the "house" will soon follow. Alexander Hamilton eloquently sums it up when he said:

> *"Without religion, morality falters. When*
> *morality falters the pandora's box of corruption,*
> *crime and decay set in to be followed by the*
> *demise of the nation."*

A weak foundation is deceptive because it appears to be strong until adversity arises. By then it is too late to remedy the problem. Jesus offers to us a parable which contrasts the "house that was built on the solid foundation and the house that was built on sand." (Luke 6:47-49)

In reading this Scripture we can see that both houses were actually built. So long as there was no adversity the house on the sand stood just as the house that was built on the rock. However, when adversity came the foundation was tested and that which was on the rock stood and that which was built on sand fell. We would do well to remember that Jesus is the author and fountainhead of our "civil liberties". To turn from His precepts of life erodes their security.

During the last several years we have consistently heard liberals interpret the First Amendment to the United States Constitution in light of secular Humanism. This excludes God from all matters of public policy and life, e.g. banning prayer in public schools or graduation, singing Christian songs at Christmas, ordering the "ten commandments" to be taken from a public building, etc. This is revisionist, illogical, and at worst, dangerous for the nation.

This type of interpretation de-stablizes the moral and social welfare of the nation by assaulting the basic ethic upon which the nation was built, i.e. the Judeo-Christian Ethic. Therefore, it is necessary that we respond to this revisionist interpretation of the Constitution as well as the liberal view of the role and relationship of the Judeo-Christian ethic in public life.

3

A Political Christian

In the early 1980's I was invited to the Christian Broadcasting Network for a seminar being held for their "partners." While there I received a clear word from the Lord that said, *one day you will work for him.* I had no idea what was meant by that. I had learned in my walk with the Lord to never interpret a "word" from the Holy Spirit in terms of human comprehension without the understanding given from the Lord.

Seven years passed when, in 1987 I began hearing rumors that Pat Robertson was considering a run for the Republican nomination for the Presidency of the United States of America. I was enthusiastic at the possibility of such an intelligent man with a strong moral background running for President.

Upon hearing that an exploratory committee was formed I promptly got myself involved. First I helped get signatures to encourage Pat to run for the nomination. As time went on and Pat formally announced his candidacy I got deeper involved in the campaign.

One day while I was studying my Bible I began to question whether I, as a Christian, should be getting actively involved in politics. As I meditated on this question I decided to pray for the Lord's guidance in this area. Should God's people be involved in politics? What does the mind of the Lord say about this?

As I continued to study my Bible I found myself in the Scriptures of Jeremiah, and I read:

> *"Then shalt thou say unto them, Because your*
> *fathers have forsaken me, saith the Lord,*
> *and have walked after other gods, and have*
> *served them, and have worshipped them, and*
> *have forsaken me, and have not kept my law;*
> *And ye have done worse than your fathers;*
> *for behold, ye walk every man after the*
> *imagination of his evil heart, that they may*
> *not hearken unto me"* Jeremiah 16:11,12.

Shortly after God spoke these words to Jeremiah, Israel found itself in the throws of defeat and bondage. I knew that idolatry provoked God to send punishment but now we see that to walk after the "imagination of his evil heart" is considered by God to be far worse.

Then I understood that America is in the depth of Secular Humanism. America had gone past the darkness of idolatry to "walk after the imagination of his evil heart." What was next for America? Judgment.

I understood that the humanist anti-Christ spirit was working in the nation through those people in government who were subject to it. What is critical is that government is like a nation's rudder which guides its' direction. Either to the land of prosperity and blessing or to the abyss of natural and spiritual bankruptcy. Thus, whoever is at the helm of the ship of State determines the destination of the nation.

Once again, I am reminded of many Christians who discourage Christian involvement in politics saying that we should pray for our leaders but don't get involved. That is a contradiction in terms.

Can you imagine government leaders who are wicked, and then respond to the call of Christ and come to know Jesus and His life's principles? What are they suppose to do? Are they to resign office so that other wicked rulers will take their place? What a ridiculous thought!

I Chronicles chapter eleven records that after the death of Saul the children of Israel "gathered themselves together and made David king."

"...Behold, we are thy bone and thy flesh. And moreover in time past, even when Saul was king, thou wast he that leddest out and broughtest in Israel: and the Lord thy God said unto thee, thou shalt feed my people Israel, and thou shalt be ruler over my people Israel".
I Chronicles 11:1,2

Their military defeats were reversed and the blessings of God was with Israel because God was with David.

"So David waxed greater and greater; for the Lord of hosts was with him" I Chronicles 11:9.

Even though God had anointed David to be king of Israel, the people had to act on the promise in order for it to come to pass. Thus, further establishing the necessity for God's people to act upon His promise in order for it to come to pass. In this situation when David was made King the people rejoiced because upon David was the blessing, anointing and presence of God to bring about victory, peace and prosperity.

It was clearly understood that in addition to being involved in Pat's campaign God wants His people to be involved in all levels of government.

Pat Announces His Candidacy

In September of 1987 Pat officially announced his candidacy for the Republican nomination for President. The wheels of the campaign went into high gear. Pat's campaign became known as a mystery campaign because a vast majority of his supporters were people who had never participated in the political process before. Therefore they were not on any records of the major political parties.

As Special Events Director for the Second Congressional District of Iowa, I had a first hand view of the demographic profile of Pat's campaign. It truly started a Populist movement.

Invariably, the vast majority of the people supporting the campaign were ordinary citizens. Mothers, fathers and children going together to the rallies, passing out campaign literature at events and even going door to door. This truly was a "family campaign."

In the fall of 1987 there was a Republican fund raiser being held at Ames, Iowa where there was to be a straw poll taken. Marlene Elwell, director of a multi-state region which included Iowa expressed the seriousness of having a good showing in the straw poll. Everyone worked late into the night rounding up support and encouraging supporters to go to the event. The response received was encouraging but it was not possible to tell if that enthusiastic support would translate into results.

The day of the event came and it was amazing. The event was a complete sell out and people had to be turned away. All the candidates were present. It was a virtual "who's who" in the Republican Party.

At one point I turned around in my front row seat and saw a "sea" of Robertson For President signs throughout the auditorium. Cheers and shouts of campaign slogans thundered throughout the arena.

When then Vice President Bush finished speaking I remember vividly how all the Robertson supporters on the ground floor/front came to express respect and well wishes in keeping with the Biblical admonition to honor governmental leaders. To our right sat the Bush supporters and you could see all their heads turning and looking at us in bewilderment. It was as if they wondered about such an enthusiastic response to a candidate they were trying to defeat.

The end of the evening came and we went to the party held by the Robertson campaign. Everyone was waiting for the results of the straw ballot. The Robertson "camp" knew that we had done well, but no one knew how well. About an hour went by and news of the results came in—Robertson had won.

This sent shockwaves throughout the world. The reason being that prior to that evening all the polls showed Pat running a distant third and sometimes fourth place in the race. Now the Robertson group was a real, viable candidate and someone to be taken seriously.

The campaign, invigorated by the unexpected victory began picking up more momentum. The appeal of the Robertson message of common sense and morality began to expand beyond the demographics of evangelical Christians.

Marlene and the Churches

During the campaign there was an effort to isolate the Robertson candidacy as being a single issue campaign with a narrow appeal. In other words, Pat was unelectable and narrow-focused.

To counter this attempt it was decided by the Robertson campaign to redirect the focus toward the secular audience and away from the evangelical base. Personally, this had given me great concern because I saw this move as turning away from Pat's main power base.

In January of 1988 I was attending a meeting for the Robertson campaign in Dallas, Texas. I shared with Marc Nuttle one of the campaign leaders, that I could present Pat an audience of 2000 people if they would let me take him into the churches. He requested that I send a note of request to the headquarters in Virginia Beach, VA. Upon my return to Cedar Rapids I sent the memo of request.

A few days later I received a telephone call informing me that in order to have my request granted I would have to persuade Marlene Elwell, the Regional Director to request the event. What made this more difficult was that I could not to tell her of my conversations with the headquarters in order to convince her to submit the request.

What could I do? I prayed. Then I made the telephone call to the state headquarters in Des Moines, Iowa. John Miller, the State Director answered the telephone. Before I could even ask to speak to Marlene he said to me, "Tony, I'm going to tell you something but it must be kept confidential."

I replied, "I will, what is it?"

He then said, "Marlene is going to ask the national office to send Pat into some Churches in Cedar Rapids. We just got done talking about it and she has not made the request to the national office yet."

I told him that I would definitely keep it confidential, and then he asked me who I wanted to speak to. Still stunned, I must have said that I was calling to see how things were going. After a brief moment the conversation closed.

Sitting back in my chair, dazed I stared up at the ceiling. I could not believe what I heard. I thought I was dreaming or something. Marlene, without a word from me had completely changed her mind.

After getting over the initial shock of the experience I knew that God was speaking to her and it was just as obvious that she was listening.

Well, the request for Pat to visit the Churches was approved and in one evening Pat was presented to two audiences totaling a number of nearly two thousand people.

After the 1988 Iowa Caucuses were over, in which Pat took second place, I went to Los Angeles, California to help with the campaign in California. As history tells it, the Super Tuesday primaries in the South proved to seal up the nomination for George Bush. Shortly thereafter Pat conceded the nomination and threw his support behind him.

Many of us who were so dedicated had a question. If Pat was going to lose, then what was his purpose running for office in the first place?

I pondered this question myself and in prayer sought the Lord's wisdom. It was not until I went back to Cedar Rapids, Iowa that I received the answer to my prayer. Pat's campaign made it acceptable for Christians to be involved in the political process and that they could have a positive impact. After all, many of the issues sensitive to Christians were endorsed by George Bush and now have come to the forefront of American political life.

Dan Quayle picked up on that theme in the 1992 election and now virtually all the Republican candidates for President as well as the recent Congress has continued to emphasize a need to return to our moral underpinnings.

Why are they so vocal? Because the American people are crying out for a return to sound moral principles. It's as though the echo of Pat's campaign is now reverberating in American politics eight years later.

The continued effect of the Robertson campaign was soon to manifest. Shortly after the election was over the movie, *"The Last Temptation of Christ"* had just been made and was being prepared for release. This movie denigrated the person of Jesus Christ.

On a set day there was a demonstration held at Universal Studios protesting the movie. The people protesting the movie arrived in waves. The numbers of people were estimated from 25,000 to 50,000. As I watched these people come to speak out I wondered to myself, *would this kind of response to a direct attack on Christ have taken place had the Robertson campaign not existed and subsequently demonstrate the positive influence and impact of the Christian voice in public affairs?*

The Christian Coalition

In 1990 the Christian Coalition was formed. When I received an invitation to attend the first national meeting entitled the *"Road To Victory Conference,"* I thought about going but was leaning against it..

One day, driving down the freeway in Los Angeles I saw an angel with his arm pointing to the east. The message was clear. I was suppose to go to the Christian Coalition Conference in Washington D.C.

The next day I got a call from a friend of mine who was a Regional Director for the Christian Coalition. She said that the Executive Director, Ralph Reed told her that Pat Robertson had been praying and that there were ten names of people who he was to personally call to ensure they were at the conference meeting in Washington D.C. My name was one of the ten. Talk about confirmation.

The number of people who attended the first *"Road to Victory Conference"* was a little over one hundred. The event in 1995 had approximately 4500 people in attendance. As of February 1996 the membership has grown to nearly two million.

There are many conservative organizations working to give people with sound moral values a voice in public policy. Leaders like Beverly LeHaye of the Concerned Women for America, Dr. James Dobson from Focus on the Family, Gary Bauer with the Family Research Council and many others are raising the standard of moral, intellectual and fiscal standards.

Although each of these and other groups work independent of each other the effect is as a "network" of righteousness and truth promoting those values, standards and policies which have consistently proved to be successful and beneficial to society.

The independent, but coordinated efforts of these groups worked together to defeat President Clinton's efforts to lift the ban on homosexuals in the military. Over 500,000 telephone calls to Congress were made. Those against lifting the ban on homosexuals in the military came in at a 10-1 ratio.

Again it was the American people who spoke against the President's efforts to turn the health care system into a socialistic bureaucracy. Big Brother was rejected.

Having seen all of these current events is encouraging. God's hand was using the Robertson campaign to set the standard for increased Christian involvement in political and governmental affairs. Through this involvement our nation can return to the foundation of moral principles and faith in God, with freedom, justice and liberty.

4

The Move to California

Time went on, the election came and went and in the fall of 1989 I found myself back in Cedar Rapids, Iowa. What a wonderful contrast between the sweet, peaceful air of Cedar Rapids and the violence and smog of Los Angeles. One afternoon, while sitting on my mother's couch I began to feel the move of God's Spirit convicting me that I should move to California.

I struggled intensely with this idea. Los Angeles was the land of earthquakes, high real estate prices, high crime, and expensive living. Cedar Rapids offered clean air, safe streets, excellent economy.

In just fifteen minutes I could either be riding my quarter horse or be in downtown Cedar Rapids on business. I remember seeing women and children walking down the sidewalk late at night without fear or harm. I was comfortable.

I was torn between the two. Live where I wanted to live or go where God wanted me to go. Additionally, I kept questioning whether I was truly hearing the mind of the Lord?

The conviction in my soul became so great I said to the Lord, *"Lord, if it is your perfect will that I go to California I will do it but if this is not you speaking to me I wouldn't touch California with a "ten foot pole."*

I then asked Him: *"Lord, I need to have a word from you."* Simultaneously, as I was speaking the telephone rang. It was a friend of mine who said, "I've got a 'word' from God for you and I'm going to be obedient and give it."

"What is it?" I asked.

She then said, "You're supposed to go to California."

I graciously thanked her and upon hanging up the telephone I collapsed on the couch. I was stunned and shocked. Not only did God answer my prayer but he was fulfilling the promise of Isaiah 65:24 where he said that he would answer our prayers while they are yet in our mouth.

Prophetic Word About the Collapse of California Real Estate

Well, I obeyed the Lord and planned to move to California. Since I was going to live there I decided to invest in real estate since the property values were accelerating to new heights.

On the day of my departure my mother took me to the airport. I got on the plane and as I waited for the door to shut and the plane to take off, the Lord told me to get off the plane. My initial thought was that the flight attendant would think I was crazy and secondly, it was unusual, to say the least.

The Lord kept persisting and so I got off the plane. Yes, the flight attendant gave a real bewildered look. Oddly enough, upon arriving in the terminal area I saw my mother and she said she found herself walking around the terminal and not knowing why. "Now I know," she said.

Going back home that night a friend called me and while we were talking he told me about a book on finances, and it (the book) discouraged buying real estate. I thought it was interesting so I kept it in my thoughts.

The next day I caught the plane to Wichita, Kansas to see some family on my way to Los Angeles. While there I went to a bookstore, and found a book on investing. When I randomly opened it the first thing my eyes saw was the statement "don't invest in real estate." At that moment I knew to take these two experiences seriously.

A day after my arrival in Los Angeles my mother called. She told me about a 700 Club Show that had a guest of Pat Robertson who said that now was not the time to buy real estate. I then knew for an absolute fact that God was telling me not to buy real estate.

Well, as we know, California real estate has taken a dramatic drop in values. Houses are being auctioned off by the hundreds. The decline started the same month that I was going to look to purchase property.

I share this experience to show that when God revealed His "word of prophecy" to me he did not force me to act. I first had to hear His word. Second, I had to believe the word. Third, there was a need to act on the *word*. So it is in the world of civic affairs and political involvement. God calls us to action but we need to respond.

God's Move On Hollywood

Upon my arrival in Los Angeles I felt that the Lord wanted me to go to one of the major studios. While there I began to pray. Then I asked the Lord what was going on. He said, *"I'm about to do a move on Hollywood. It's not the media that is wicked, it is who has controlled it. There is such a tide of moral conservatism in America that those who maintain moral integrity will ride the wave to success but those who will not shall fall into ruin."*

Since that day we have seen the number of family-friendly films increase. We have seen the Federal government, responding to the concerns of parents, move to encourage Hollywood to reduce violence, profanity and sex in the media. We have seen 25,000-50,000 people demonstrate against a movie that was blasphemous. And there is more to come.

The movies which have become the most successful are by and large substantive. For example, *"Indiana Jones The Last Crusade"* which vilified blasphemy; *"Honey I Shrunk The Kids"* which was a fun family film. *"Gettysburg"* and many others.

1995 has seen the greatest effort on the part of the American people to shake the entertainment industry to their senses. The American people have said that "trash T.V." sex, violence and profanity on television and films are not acceptable and they want something done about it. This is directly reflected by the concerns that government leaders and politicians are expressing. After all they simply respond to that which pushes the "public button."

In the beginning of 1996 there was a conference on this subject held at Paramount studios. Studio executives, producers, directors, Senators and Congressmen as well as actors and the general public were in attendance. It was really amazing to see such a serious discussion held which extolled the virtues of responsibility.

The people are speaking and the entertainment industry and government are listening. According to a recent MTV poll of those eighteen years of age and younger, over 90% want less sex on television. A USA Today/CNN/Gallup poll found that 80% of respondents were concerned about the moral breakdown as related to the media.

What I find interesting is that during the Golden Age of Hollywood there was no need for government involvement. There was no talk of censorship. Why? Because the Church and the entertainment industry worked together to provide quality films and programming while at the same time maintaining creative freedom. Their focus was based on moral decency and creative freedom.

God's move comes through people when they pray and when they act on their faith and moral convictions.

5

Moses and Politics

Moses Could Have Been Pharaoh

As we read the story of Moses and how he was saved from the water by Pharaoh's daughter we see that it was the Lord who set him in Pharaoh's house.

The Lord set Moses in the position of political pre-eminence in Eqypt. Then after learning of his heritage and seeing an Egyptian taskmaster beating an Israelite he killed the Egyptian. This ultimately lead to his expulsion into the desert where he learned how to be a shepherd. This prepared him to lead the nation of Israel into the Promised Land and to shepherd them before, during, and after the deliverance.

As we can see, Moses was God's instrument in delivering Israel outside the realm of internal Egyptian politics. Some people may see this as the Lord setting precedent that God's people and God's move in a nation are outside internal politics. The contrary is actually true.

The reasons why are numerous. Moses was put into Pharaoh's house by God Himself and ultimately this positioning led to his elevation in the line of royalty which possibly could have led to him being Pharaoh.

Moses' descent from Egyptian royalty was not by the hand of God but rather by his own hand when he murdered the Egyptian. Remember, Moses committed murder. God would not cause someone to commit murder in order to accomplish His divine plan. However, God does take the "chaff" of the lawlessness of our life, and through repentance and purification, uses those circumstances to bring forth His perfect will in our life and the lives around us.

Through Moses' error and sin he was cast into the desert where he ultimately learned how to shepherd people as well as lead them.

When Moses confronted Pharaoh he honored his position by approaching his throne in telling him to let the Israelites go, rather than stirring up rebellion. In this same manner Jesus honored the position of the Pharisees. He told the people to obey them because they sit in Moses' seat. However he cautioned them not to live as they do. (Matthew 23:1,2)

Moses confronted the office holder and not the institution. He rebuked Pharaoh's policy and not his authority. The office holder, Pharaoh, was confronted in order for him to change policy not only for the good of Israel but for the good of all of the people he ruled. Remember, Pharaoh's hard heart brought the plagues upon all of Egypt. Pharaoh did not have to be replaced, but rather his policies had to be changed. The position of Pharaoh was used for several hundred years as a blessing to multitudes of people, Egyptian and otherwise.

A good example of this is with regard to Joseph and the interpretation of Pharaoh's dream. Through the office of Pharaoh Joseph delivered the interpretation of the dreams and not only was Egypt saved from the seven years of famine but the entire known world in that area came to Egypt to be fed.(Genesis 41)

In confronting Pharoah's policies God, through Moses, took the opportunity to contrast the power of God and the power of Pharaoh. As God told Moses, he used Pharoah in order to demonstrate his power and to humble Egypt so that the whole world would know that there is the true and living God in Israel.

Never did we hear Moses or the Lord say that the political system of Egypt was, in and of itself, evil or bad. But rather we heard that the policies carried out by the political institution was evil and an affront to God. This government office was ultimately used to set Israel free.

What if?

One day while driving down the freeway in Los Angeles I saw in my mind a picture of Mount Sinai. At the bottom I saw Moses tending his sheep. The upper portion of the mountain was enshrouded in the cloud of God's presence. The top of the mountain was inflamed with the illuminating glow of fire and lightning. Thunder reverberated across the sky causing the mountain and ground to tremble.

I saw Moses look up to the top of Mount Sinai staring in awe at this sight. He climbed to the top. In great fear and trembling he beheld a sight that could not be comprehended. A bush engulfed by a flame yet not consumed.

He heard the voice of the Lord speaking from the midst of the bush. Slowly but deliberately the Lord spoke with the gentleness and authority of His great love and power saying: *"Moses...Moses...Moses"*

Moses replied, "Here am I Lord."

Again the Lord spoke, *"Take off thy shoes from off thy feet for the ground upon which you stand is holy ground."*

Moses, shaking and trembling, quickly took off his sandals all the while continuing to stare at the bush which was burning but not consumed. He fell to his knees in worship and fear of the Lord, hiding his face from the brightness of the Holy fire.

He then asked the Lord, "Lord, why have you not heard the cries of your people?"

The Lord replied, *"Surely I have heard the cries of my people. I have now come to deliver them from bondage."*

God then spoke again, *"I will send you Moses. I shall put my words in your mouth and my power through your staff. Now go to Pharaoh, Moses. Tell him that I said to 'let my people go.'"*

Moses stood upright on his feet and in a firm but puzzling voice replied, ""I don't know Lord... I don't think that God's people should be involved in politics..."

My immediate response to this vision, if you will, was a mixture of laughter and seriousness. The Lord made clear to me that this was to show me what could have happened had Moses possessed the same attitude about setting the Hebrews free that many Christians have about getting involved in civic affairs.

Moses' staff was God's instrument of His power. Today the office of civil government is the staff of God's power in America to bring deliverance, justice, peace and prosperity.

If Moses had thought God's people should not be involved in politics, the Hebrews would possibly have remained in bondage for an indefinite period of time and the Bible, as we know it, would not have been written.

We would be deprived of God's lessons of redemption as we see through the life of Moses who was exiled for killing the Egyptian. Yet this "skeleton" in his "closet" did not lead to his destruction but through the redeeming hand of God it propelled him into the desert to learn to shepherd sheep which ultimately prepared him to shepherd the "sheep of God's pasture," the Israelites. What a beautiful example of restoration and redemption.

Thank God, Moses did not reject His call to "politics." He heard, he obeyed and the whole nation of Israel was set free. Egypt saw the salvation of God, the Covenant between God and His people was established, the prophecies of the Messiah were proclaimed, and the whole world was given a legal system which has brought justice and equity to mankind.

The Lord called Moses to confront Pharaoh. It is beneficial for us to make note of several points of interest. First, the Israelites cried to the Lord for deliverance. Second, the Lord heard their cry and manifested Himself in earth to set the date of deliverance. Third, and very crucial, is that God invaded the realm of Egyptian politics through the hand of man to bring the "policy change" which set the Israelites free using Egypt as an example of God's power.

God did not have to use the hand of Moses to deliver the nation of Israel. He could have softened Pharaoh's heart and spoken to him to let the people go.

God did speak directly to one Pharaoh of Egypt (Genesis 12:11-20). The story begins with Abraham going to Egypt to avoid the famine. Being afraid of the Egyptians he and Sarah lied to Pharaoh saying that she was his sister. Pharaoh took her to himself and God sent a plague upon Egypt until it was made known to Pharaoh that Sarah was Abraham's wife.

God spoke directly in telling Pharaoh to release Sarah back to Abraham. In like manner God could have spoken to Pharaoh Ramases II. Instead, God gave him over to what he was: *Hard hearted.*

In this we see that God established a precedent for Himself to speak directly to the kings in authority. Now, we ask, why did God choose the deliverance of Israel to be accomplished through the hand of the man Moses?

In doing so God was accomplishing a three fold purpose. First, to set Israel free, Secondly, God was establishing that His deliverance comes only by His Spirit. (Zechariah 4:6) Third, even though the deliverance of the Lord comes by the unction of the Holy Spirit, it is applied through the hand of man as He gives authority, wisdom and knowledge to achieve the goal.

How does this relate to the political realm? We are to know that the arm of the Lord moves through mankind to bring deliverance and blessing to the oppressed through the man or woman of God.

Egypt Blessed Through The Deliverance Of Israel

In the case of Ramases II Pharaoh of Egypt, God established that man was to be involved in the deliverance and ministry of God's divine judgment and truth.

God's working through Moses was also intended to reveal Himself to the Egyptians and the rest of the world. Through the Israelites the world would come to know the true and living God.

"And the Egyptians shall know that I am the Lord,
when I have gotten me honor upon Pharaoh, upon
his chariots, and upon his horsemen" Exodus 4:18.

Pharaoh and all of Egypt was the predominant power in the known world. Thus, when Pharaoh's vast numbers of soldiers, chariots and horsemen were overthrown by God, Egypt then knew that God was God. The word of God's destruction of Pharoah's armies spread throughout the world.

What most people do not realize is that Egypt was used by God to protect Jesus when Herod went on his murderous rampage (Matthew 2:13-15) Subsequently, Egypt became one of the greatest centers of Christianity in the world.

In the early days of Church history there were five centers of Christian authority and life—Jerusalem, Antioch, Constantinople, Rome, and Alexandria. The Egyptian Christians were later to become known as Coptic Orthodox.

Many of the great saints of Christendom came out of Egypt such as St. Antony of Egypt. He was the founder of the monastic movement whose life demonstrated spiritual warfare and the gifts of the Holy Spirit. St. Athanasius of Egypt who spearheaded the defense of the doctrine of the nature of Christ as being "homoousias" (of the same nature as the Father).

God Delivers Israel Apart From Internal Political Involvement

Some people may justify non political-governmental involvement by God's people by pointing to the fact that God used Moses to deliver Israel from bondage after he was out of political authority.

We need to reference the primary principle of biblical interpretation. Namely, that every Scripture must be interpreted in its context.

The context of the story of Moses shows that God purposely sought to distinguish between the authority and power of human ability personified through the Egyptian priests, Jannus and Jambres (II Timothy 3:8), the armies of Egypt, and the authority of Pharaoh for the purpose of demonstrating to the world for time immemorial that God is God and there is no hope nor power outside of Him.

The Scriptures document God's move within the context of human government as being in His perfect will and not in His permissive will as we see in the lives of Joseph, Jehosaphat, Daniel, etc.

We can see that even when God moves in a sovereign way He still uses the hand of man joining with Him to bring about His kingdom on earth.

God moved on Pharaoh by the miracles done through Moses. A man whom Pharaoh did not esteem and considered him stricken from the land.

Thus, even though Moses did not occupy public office and God was moving in a supernatural way, the Lord still caused

Moses to engage the political powers in order to bring about the deliverance of Israel. We can learn from this example.

God Gives Wisdom to Moses Through Jethro

Jethro, Moses father-in-law, saw how Moses was wearing himself out in judging the issues of the children of Israel. He, being given God's wisdom, spoke to Moses and suggested that judges be appointed by him. The smaller matters would be judged by them and the more difficult matters would be judged by him (Moses).

Moses
Rulers of thousands
Rulers of hundreds
Rulers of fifties
Rulers of tens
Exodus 18:25, 26

Note the qualifications of the "rulers." They had to be capable administrators of the office. They had to be men of truth, who "feared God" and hated covetousness which perverts the eyes of wisdom and judgment.(Exodus 18:21)

God instructed Moses to choose men with these qualifications rather than doing it himself. This He did to accomplish a two fold purpose. The first being to fulfill the immediate need. The second was to establish a model after which future generations are to exercise their authority to select leaders and the criteria upon which to base the decisions.

Could you imagine if our governmental and civic leaders had the kind of qualifications that God established? I dare say that our national debt would be virtually eliminated. The poor in our country would be diminished due to more effective government. The billions spent on A.I.D.S. could be saved because sexual perversion would not be endorsed and promoted by government and society. Role models would be moral and honorable resulting in a higher standard of behavior and focus for America's youth and adults.

Crime would be greatly reduced because true justice would be meted out to criminals. Victims of crime would be given proper restitution. Government decisions would be based upon the merits of the positions without the influence of special interest groups.

Their eyes of judgment would be clear. Their decisions would be driven by what is right, "pork barrel" spending would be greatly reduced or eliminated. Can you imagine the billions of dollars that the United States taxpayer would save? Can you imagine the positive ripple effect on the strength of the United States economy with all those billions of dollars being converted into savings and consumer spending? Can you imagine federal, state and local governments being able to balance their budgets by not being subject to gross waste and fraud? Imagine how low the interest rates would be if the government was not in competition with the business sector in borrowing money.

Some may call such a goal only a dream. But since God commanded Moses to pursue these type of men He is implying that they were available. Jethro was anointed by God to give Moses this counsel. This counsel went to the heart of Moses and he implemented the recommendations. If the qualifications of the "Rulers" were idealistic then why would Jethro, a man from the desert make such a recommendation? Why would God give such wisdom to Jethro to share with Moses and why would Moses implement the suggestions? Since Moses implemented the recommendations then evidently he found men who met those honorable qualifications.

Therefore, far be it from us to say that such men and women do not exist in America. They do. Some do not take public service as a serious calling. In many instances these people are discouraged from stepping out into the public arena. This discouragement may come by their own perception of being incapable and others may be discouraged by the erroneous teaching of some Christian leaders that "God's people" should not be involved in politics. Yet others are not elected to positions of public service because those people of like mind simply do not participate in the political process.

Through the involvement of God's people, guided by the "mind and wisdom of Christ," liberty and truth guide a nation in answer to the prayers of God's people. Obedience to God is the fountainhead of freedom. Rejection of the statutes of God is bondage.

In her book *"Jesus Called Her Mother"* Dee Jepsen quotes Mary Ann Detrama who says, *"...Truly the only real freedom is complete and absolute submission to God's will..."*

As we read the Scriptures and the history of God's relationship with mankind we consistently see that except for isolated instances, God answers prayer through the involvement of His people.

A most interesting demonstration of this principle can be seen when the Israelites were at the Red Sea, Pharaoh was approaching from the rear and Moses cried to God for help. The Lord's response was not what was expected by Moses.

"And the Lord said unto Moses, 'Wherefore criest thou unto me? Speak unto the children of Israel that they go forward: But lift thou up thy rod, and stretch out thine hand over the sea, and divide it: and the children of Israel shall go on dry ground through the midst of the sea'" Exodus 14:15, 16.

We can see that God made provision of His authority and power but in order for Moses (and us) to experience the manifestation and benefit of such power and authority it must be applied through faith and corresponding action.

When Moses lifted up the staff and stretched it out over the sea he linked heaven and earth. He acknowledged the power of the Lord in lifting up the staff toward heaven and then he applied this power and authority in the earth when he stretched out the staff over the Red Sea. John Chrysostom points out that these two actions formed a cross. He lifted it up and stretched it out.

The parting and the closing of the Red Sea was done by God through the hand of a man who was committed to serving Him and His people (Exodus 14:26-31).

Moses stretched out his hand over the Red Sea. Once to open and the other to close it. He opened it for the Israelites' safe passage and closed it to cut off Pharaoh.

When God fearing people extend their hand to vote for qualified and honorable men and women they open the door for them to bring reason, logic and godly principles to government.

To those who do not adhere to sound moral judgments a believer's vote will close the "Red Sea" upon their political career disabling them to effect negative influence upon society.

The Position of Governmental Office Is Amoral

We can conclusively see that the office of "Pharaoh," as with all government offices, was amoral. The position of Pharaoh enforced and carried out the moral or immoral policies of the person or persons who occupy the reins of power. The question of whether that office is used for good or bad is completely up to the one who has the reins of its' power. In America today, it is the choice of the governed as to who possesses the reins of authority.

We may do well to remember the admonition of President Kennedy in his inaugural speech in 1961 when he said, "*...God's work must truly be our own...*".

6

David and Goliath

The biblical story of David and Goliath has inspired people through the ages. It has challenged them to accomplish the impossible, defeat the unbeatable, and attain the unattainable.

However, there is another lesson that we can learn from this story of a young man's commitment to God and his people. Namely, that faith and action are the integral elements which provide for the victory.

David, a young man confronted a huge Philistine warrior named Goliath. The giant had taunted the armies of Israel and struck fear in their hearts.

When Goliath issued the proposal that one man of Israel would fight him in a winner take all battle, no one stepped forward to engage him in battle. David, upon hearing of this, approached the king to offer himself as Israel's warrior. He told the king that when a lion and a bear attacked his sheep God delivered them into his hand to kill them. God would do the same thing with this uncircumcised Philistine who dared defy the armies of the living God.

Why was David so bold? Because he possessed the two keys to confidence and victory. First he had a personal relationship with God, and second he was committed to his responsibilities.

David prepared for his battle with Goliath being established upon a four principle foundation. Goliath was an enemy of God because he worshipped pagan gods. Therefore he was not in a covenant relationship with God. This is why David referred to Goliath as an "uncircumcised Philistine" (I Samuel 17:26).

The source of David's strength came from his faith in God. Having experienced God's sovereign power in delivering his sheep from the bear and the lion he knew God would do the same with this Philistine who defied God's armies.

At this point it may be beneficial to note that David's defense of the sheep did not manifest through idle prayer in the security of his father's house leaving the sheep to the "will of God." David, had his relationship with God founded on the solid rock of his love and obedience to Him. He was diligent to carry out his responsibilities to the best of his ability. He was resolved that nothing was going to rob him of what was entrusted to him. He was a young man of diligence and responsibility. He could be trusted with the gifts of God.

Thus, when the lion and the bear sought to steal his sheep he put forth all of his effort in his natural ability while at the same time being established in his faith in God. The Lord honored David by delivering the lion and bear into his hands for their destruction.

David had a plan to successfully attack Goliath. Note that the Scriptures record that when David went to meet Goliath he possessed five stones. Many Bible teachers have tried to spiritualize the meaning of the five stones. Simply put, they represented David's attitude toward his task. He was not going to be so presumptuous of his own ability as to think that only one stone would be needed. He resolved that in doing his part he carried five stones because of his intent to persevere. If the first stone missed he was going to throw another, and another until he had the victory.

The five stones represented David's commitment to battle and fervent commitment to fight until the battle was won. He was going to prepare himself completely, he was going to apply himself completely and he was going to trust God completely.

Can you imagine what the political spectrum, families, and businesses would look like if Godly people had this type of attitude and faith in God toward their responsibilities? I dare say that the divorce rate would drastically decline and along with it the crime rate because children would be home being built up emotionally, spiritually and intellectually by the security of a sound family environment. Commitment to responsibility would also increase business efficiency.

Governmental leaders would be more effective. They would be single purposed in seeking to accomplish that which is moral ethical and productive for the city, state and country. This attitude and focus would not be swayed by temporal gain but by eternal truth. Thus the policies and positions established would be those which would bring forth the greatest good for the nation and the world.

It was God who was going to bless the work of David and deliver the "uncircumcised Philistine" into his hands. We see a recurring theme that God is establishing throughout the story of David and Goliath, and throughout the whole of Scriptures themselves. When a person has set out to do that which is approved in the sight of God whether it be the slaying of Goliath, protecting the unborn, bringing forth moral standards of behavior, delivering the oppressed from the oppressor we see that when prayer is joined with actions, victory and freedom result.

However, when there is prayer without action or action without prayer potential disaster awaits. For example, the Scriptures record that:

> *"And the Philistine drew near morning and evening,*
> *and presented himself forty days"* I Samuel 17:16.

Goliath kept making this proposition morning and night for forty days. Saul and all his armies were terrified of Goliath (that's probably why forty days went by without Israel answering the challenge). I believe that it is reasonable to assume that Saul and the armies of Israel offered up prayer regarding this situation. In light of this I find it interesting that after praying for forty days and no one taking the challenge of Goliath God did not remove the Philistine threat. Thus, at that point, their prayer was without fruit because they did not put forth corresponding action.

However, God did answer their prayer, but it came in the form of sending someone who would coordinate their prayer of faith with their 100% effort in their actions to effect the victory. God gave them David. Goliath did not go away. God did not strike him dead by a heart attack or a bolt of lightning from heaven. Rather, God was establishing the principle that prayer and faith must coordinate with actions.

The results of the battle between David and Goliath is known to all. God blessed the labor of David's hands as he exercised the abilities and resources he had. Totally and completely trusting in the Lord and giving him complete credit for the victory.

Hear what David says to Goliath about how he was going to kill him:

"Then said David to the Philistine, Thou
comest to me with a sword, and with a spear,
and with a shield: but I come to thee in the
name of the Lord of hosts, the God of the
armies of Israel, whom thou has defied.

This day will the Lord deliver thee into
mine hand; and I will smite thee, and take
thine head from thee; and I will give the
carcasses of the host of the Philistines
this day unto the birds of the air, and
to the wild beasts of the earth, that the
earth may know that there is a God in Israel."

I Samuel 17:45,46

Although David completely and thoroughly prepared himself with the weapons of warfare with which he was proficient he attributes to the Lord as being the source of his strength and the benefactor of His victory. While the Philistines looked at their natural abilities as the source of their power and strength, David viewed his ability as the tools, and the instruments, through which the Spirit of the Lord will provide the victory.

David's abilities and labors combined with prayer and faith in God has served to be an encouragement to all mankind who has found itself overwhelmed by the forces of opposition. By hard work, prayer and faith in God nothing shall be impossible to those who believe.

In order for God to move in the supernatural we need to put forth a one hundred per cent effort in the natural. Applying all of our gifts and talent God has given us.

This is what the cripple man did who sat by the pool of Siloam. Once a year the angel of the Lord would stir the water and the first one in would be healed of their malady. What I find interesting is that this man had been there for thirty eight years. Since he was a paralytic he virtually had no chance of being the first into the pool. However, he was doing everything he knew to do. Hoping against hope. What happens? He receives more than he expected. He encountered the God of the angel that stirs the waters. He was not only healed but he has now become a testimony in the Holy Scriptures becoming an example and encouragement for unwavering faith. Lastly, he applied his faith in one direction, i.e. the pool of Siloam but God delivered the answer from the hand of his Son.

Government:
"David's Sling" For God's People Today

Governmental authority and institutions can be the "sling" of God's people. A weapon that has the potential to be used to slay the "Goliaths" of poverty, injustice, immorality, crime and corruption.

When government authority is in the hands of the unrighteous and immoral these institutions can be the instruments of oppression in the hands of the oppressor. For example, one person in 1962, through the judicial court system was able to eradicate God from the classroom. As we know, the effects were devastating. In 1973, one person's legal action opened the door for the national consent to the death of over thirty million children. If so much evil has been done by one person's use of the governmental institutions, how much good could a multitude of people do in bringing about moral and sound public policy? These institutions are given by God to bring about those policies and laws which are healthy and good for the nation

The early colonists found themselves confronting the "Goliath" of the British Monarchy. They responded by committing their lives and fortunes to the cause of freedom covered by prayer and commitment to Jesus Christ. The results? "David" wins again.

It is for this reason some of the Founding Fathers such as John Jay, the first Chief Justice of the Supreme Court said that *"this was a Christian nation and that it was the duty of the people to elect Christian leaders..." "It is preferable that Christians should be preferred to govern."*

The intent was not to exclude a particular person from holding public office, but rather to ensure that the Christian tenants of faith, morals and conduct are irrevocably imputed as the foundations of government and public life and policy.

One of the most profound statements on the issue of Christian activity in politics and government was spoken by Alexander Hamilton...

> *"Of all the dispositions and habits which*
> *lead to political prosperity, religion and*

morality are indispensable supports...Reason
and experience both forbid us to expect that
national morality can prevail in exclusion of
religious principle... "

Samuel Adams said:
"When one loses virtue, the law of liberty is soon to follow. There was
no difference between political service and spiritual activities."

As we consider the question of Christian involvement in politics let us keep in mind that when David offered to encounter Goliath, he did not pray that God would independently slay Goliath. Instead He used the weaponry available to him and having been skilled in their use, he committed to God his works and the victory was secured.

David had a plan. He would strike Goliath with the stone, cut off Goliath's head with his own sword and then destroy all the armies of the Philistines.

If David never picked up the sling, Goliath would not have been slain and Israel would not have been made free. David would not have been King and Solomon would not have been King of Israel. The Church would not possess the benefit of the blessings God bestowed through the hand and wisdom of both David and Solomon.

David picked up his sling to slay the Philistine giant, Goliath who threatened Israel. Let us pick up the "sling" of the political process that the Founding Fathers procured for us by the Grace and guidance of Providence to secure a healthy, prosperous and peaceful future for ourselves and our posterity.

7

Solomon, Bathsheba & Nathan—the Prophet

The story of Solomon, King of Israel demonstrates to us the critical importance of God's people being involved in government affairs.

During David's reign God promised him that Solomon would rule and reign on his throne and that it would be Solomon who would fulfill David's dream of building the house of the Lord.

> *"Behold a son shall be born to thee, who shall*
> *be a man of rest; and I will give him rest from*
> *all his enemies round about; for his name shall*
> *be Solomon, and I will give peace and quietness*
> *unto Israel in his days"* I Chronicles 22:9.

David had actually received the prophetic word of the Lord whereby Solomon was the divinely chosen man to be king of

Israel succeeding David, his father. God further tells David that through his reign there will be peace from all of Israel's enemies for such is the name Solomon, which means "peaceful."

As the story of Solomon demonstrates, the promises of God are conditional upon the choices and actions of the people to whom the promise is given.

Let's focus on the time period at which David's death is about to occur. David is sick in bed and unbeknown to him Adonijah attempts to usurp the inheritance of the throne and begins to proclaim himself to be David's successor. He even begins the celebration. He killed the sheep, oxen and cattle. He called his friends to celebrate his ascension to the throne.

Now enters the prophet Nathan. It is interesting to note that in this Scriptural text (I Kings 1:1 et al) Nathan was referred to by his spiritual position and relationship with God and David the king. Talk about mixing politics and religion. God's endorsement of such cannot be any more clear.

Nathan, through his office as a Prophet, the gifts and favor of God, combined with loyalty to his king, had access to the "first family" of Israel. Herein rests Nathan's effectiveness and ultimately the welfare of the nation of Israel, and the whole of Judaism and Christianity which I will soon point out.

When Nathan heard what Adonijah was doing he quickly developed a strategy to defeat him and ensure that Solomon would be king. Nathan spoke to Bathsheba and she heard the words of the Prophet. He first reminded her of the prophetic word of God that Solomon was to be king. He then informs her of Adonijah's plan to take the throne. He then shared with her his plan and she agreed to it. Consequently, Nathan's plan proved successful and Solomon was anointed king by David just as David promised Bathsheba by the word of the Lord. (I Kings 1:29, 30)

God's promise to Israel and the world was nearly denied because Adonijah almost succeeded in becoming king had it not been for a man of God getting involved in governmental affairs.

As it was with Nathan the Prophet so it is with Christian involvement in government. Like Nathan, Christians today need to act on the knowledge they have and the faith they possess. This will bring about effective government and moral strength to the society. Inaction brings deprivation of God's blessings.

Nathan the Prophet, through his spiritual relationship with God and his life of fasting and prayer inherently knew the importance of asserting himself in political matters. He knew that God did not want Adonijah to be King. He applied all his mental capability with prayer to plan the overthrow of Adonijah's plans. His shrewd thinking, planning and actions succeeded.

What If Solomon Wasn't King?

Had the Prophet of God not acted upon his convictions Solomon would not have been king. Israel would have been under the hand of one who was immature and self serving. The consequences could have been disastrous.

What if Nathan the Prophet did not get involved in government affairs? Would we have the Book of Proverbs, Song of Solomon, and Ecclesiastes which gives us wisdom and a perspective on life? What would have been the fate of the little child over whom the two women fought? (I Kings 3:18-28) What would have become of the nation of Israel who lived in peace and prosperity for so many years under Solomon's reign?

The Throne of David

If God did not intend for His people to be involved in politics then why did He promise David that his children would always be on the throne of Israel if they obeyed the commandments of God?

> *"And if thou (Solomon) wilt walk before me, as David thy father walked, in integrity of heart, and in uprightness to do according to all that I have commanded thee, and wilt keep my statutes and my judgments...Then I will establish the throne of thy kingdom upon Israel for ever, as I promised to David thy father, saying, There shall not fail thee a man upon the throne of Israel"* I Kings 9:4, 5.

As our salvation is dependent upon our active response to the promise of eternal life through Jesus Christ so is the nation's well being contingent upon the choice of her leaders. Will they choose the path that leads to health and prosperity?

The nation of Israel experienced this when, after being freed from Egypt, they were promised the land of "milk and honey." However, God put a condition upon it. They had to go into the land and take it from the inhabitants. God promised His favor if they put forth their labor.

The Lord through the Prophet Isaiah reiterates this same principle:

*"If ye be willing and obedient ye shall
eat the good of the land"* Isaiah 1:19, 20.

Finally, if God's people were not to be involved in government only the wicked and ignorant would be left to govern our country and influence the world. Let's always be reminded of the life of Nathan the Prophet who got involved in politics and affected world history...for the good.

8

Daniel

Daniel was a man committed to worship God, and he was enabled by His gifts to serve the king. Why is he important in understanding the mind of Christ regarding Christians in politics?

One evening God gave the king a dream. This caused him great trouble because he could not remember it and yet he knew it was of significant importance.

The king became so frustrated that none of his "wise men" and astrologers could tell him the dream and its' interpretation he put a death sentence on all of them. Hearing of this Daniel took action and sought the counsel and wisdom of God. Upon receiving it he blessed God and revealed the dream and its interpretation to the king.

Thus, the king spared their lives and Daniel was further established in the empire as a man of great wisdom and knowledge. This led the king to acknowledge the Lordship of the Hebrew God.

As much as God's gifts were evident, Daniel still had to assert himself before the king and apply the gifts he was given. To have done this he had to possess confidence in his relationship with God, knowing that the Lord would grant him knowledge of the king's dream and the interpretation.

Through the dream and the gifts of God working through Daniel the Lord engaged the enemy to battle in the spiritual and political realm simultaneously. The war in the spiritual realm took place when the demon inspired astrologers, "wise men", etc. encountered the manifestation of the living God when He sent the dream to the king and the interpretation and knowledge of it to Daniel.

However, as it is throughout the Scriptures, God's actions in the history of human events has a basic two fold purpose. The first is to address the immediate need and the second is to establish eternal principals as noted below:

1. Discrediting the Astrologers, wise men, magicians, etc. of Babylon. Thus, demonstrating that all sources of wisdom and knowledge other than God are useless and unprofitable.

2. The reality of the true and living God of Daniel was revealed to Nebuchadnezzar and through him the whole Babylonian empire. Here we see the vast impact that one single person who loves God can have in the affairs of mankind.

3. Saving the lives of the wise men, astrologers, etc. as well as Daniel himself could lead to the salvation of others who are influenced by these men.

4. Favor was extended to the Hebrews while in captivity. This established that God is not bound by our limitations.

5. Understanding and wisdom given to Daniel demonstrated that God reigns in the kingdoms of man—no matter how great or small they are.

6. God confronts evil through the lives of men in government. Subsequently, this leads to the elevation of Daniel as well as other men of God to positions of great power and authority. This provided excellence of service to the king and prosperity to the Jews. Here God establishes a model for His people to follow.

7. Contemporary Christians can see through Daniel that God's people can effect positive change for the nation. This brings forth the blessing of God as they worship and live by His statutes.

   a. This change comes through God's Spirit working with man as he applies his natural abilities in conjunction with the use of the gift of God.

   b. God, knowing the beginning from the end, established this Scripture to testify that it is through political involvement of God's people unctioned by His wisdom and truth of His Holy Spirit that God's "will be done on earth as it is in heaven..."

   c. Prayer with corresponding action will bring God's answer. Daniel prayed, God answered and Daniel applied what he received from God.

   d. It is God's will for His people to be in positions of leadership and authority.

After all, it was only through the supernatural gifting that Daniel was in a political position to have access to the king. This positioned him to be able to reveal the dreams and their interpretation to him (Daniel 1:17;2:47). This concluded in the Babylon Empire rejecting idol worship and bowing their knee to the God of Israel.

God could have spoken to the king in any way that He wanted but He chose to use Daniel. God knew that the king would elevate Daniel and He knew and ordained that Daniel would recommend the other three young men to be put in positions of authority over provinces.

"Then Daniel requested of the king, and he set Shadrach, Meshach, and Abednego, over the affairs of the province of Babylon; but Daniel sat in the gate of the king" Daniel 2:49.

What was the purpose? To rule and reign in the affairs of the king and provinces bringing justice judgment and equity to the empire. What a paradox, the captives have become the ruler over the captors. Such is the greatness of God.

Thus, we see again that God expressly wills His people to be involved in the political civic affairs of man through which He can bring truth and blessing through the knowledge of Him. There is no freedom outside of obedience to the living God.

Nebuchadnezzar Loses Sight and Gains It Again

In the fourth chapter of the Book of Daniel we read about Nebuchadnezzar relating his experience when he had another dream from the Lord which no one could interpret but Daniel.

This troubled Daniel because it was a dream of God's judgment against Nebuchadnezzar who had set himself above God. The dream was also given so that he would come to know once and for all, that it is God who rules in the affairs and kingdoms of man.

The judgment against him was that due to his pride and arrogance he would roam the fields like an animal. After the judgment was fulfilled and his right mind returned, God established him in his kingdom and he then did know that it is God who rules in the affairs of man (Daniel 4:32).

This judgment and the consumate restoration of the king was due to Daniel's unwavering commitment to the Lord God of Israel and to the King. Yes, I say the king. Sometimes loyalty and love are called upon to say things that are not comfortable but are necessary to the general health of the person to whom those things are to be said and done.

"Faithful are the wounds of a friend but deceitful is the flattery of an enemy" Proverbs 27:6.

Daniel's commitment to God and king caused him to speak the truth regardless of the consequences. He told him what he needed to hear and not what the king wanted to hear. Such is the act of a true statesman. Unfortunately, not enough statesmen are holding government offices.

Like Nebuchadnezzar, our government leaders need loyal people to give them Godly counsel with the wisdom and understanding of God's Spirit as well as being ready to tell their constituents and superiors what they needed to hear instead of what they wanted to hear. This is the example set by Daniel's relationship with God and king.

In America there are many "Daniels" who, if elected to public office, could bring forth justice and prosperity for America and the world.

9

Do You Feel "Led"?

Many people today use the phrase *"I don't feel led"* to justify not doing something that they know should be done. By this they attempt to remove the burden of responsibility and obedience.

Most of the time the Lord does not speak to us through our "feelings." He speaks directly through the Scriptures as illumined by the Holy Spirit and through the conviction of the conscience.

One case in point were the three young children of Israel who lived during the time of Daniel, (Daniel, chapter three). Their names were Shadrach, Meshach and Abednego. Most likely they did not intend to confront the political system. However, when King Nebuchadnezzar required everyone to worship the golden image he built they would not comply. The report that the young men refused to bow their knee to the image infuriated the king and propelled the young men into conflict with the government.

The natural consequences of obedience to God will take the believer into political conflict when government policies are in contradiction to the will of God as did happen not only with these three young men but also with Daniel.

Shadrach, Mishech and Abednego did not know if the Lord was going to save them from the fiery furnace or let them burn as martyrs. They simply resolved to remain faithful to Him and not worship the image while remaining loyal to the king (Dan.3:16-18).

During the confrontation the young men kept referring to Nebuchadnezar as "king." Their purpose was to establish that at no time did these young men dishonor Nebuchadnezzar as the head of governmental authority. The king's authority was challenged when it infringed on the honor due only to God.

In essence an anti-christ type spirit had entered into the realm of governmental affairs. When this imposition threatened the true honor due only to God then it was challenged by God through men of God.

God honored the challenge. By this He established the validity for Christians becoming involved in the political arena. Since the people of Daniel's day did not have the choice of government their involvement came when government tried to usurp the honor due God. Civil disobedience, if you will, just as the three young men did.

God supernaturally delivered them from the fire. Subsequently the entire kingdom of Nebuchadnezzar was committed to worshipping the God of Shadrach, Meshech and Abednego.

Abraham and Lot

The story of Abraham and Lot is a prime example of a godly man taking action based upon what he knew should be done. When Abraham's nephew, Lot, was taken prisoner Abraham did not sit back in his tent and pray for Lot's deliverance. He did three important things.

He previously built a strong relationship with God, fortified in faith by prayer and alms. Second, he prepared himself to the best of his ability and effectiveness to protect and defend against real or potential enemies. Third, when the threat manifested he applied all of his skill and resources to bring about the deliverance of Lot, the captives and their possessions.

Abraham combined the two ingredients required for success in this life. He had a strong relationship with God and he was a man of preparation and action. One without the other would have been the formula for disaster not only for Lot but for the promise made to Abraham.

We can hear the words of Melchizedek upon seeing Abraham after Lot was delivered:

"And he (Melchizedek) blessed him (Abraham), and said, Blessed be Abram of the most high God, possessor of heaven and earth; And blessed be the most high God, which hath delivered thine enemies into thy hand. And he (Abraham) gave him (Melchizedek) tithes of all he had" Genesis 14:17-24.

Melchizidek came to Abraham AFTER the battle to free Lot. Communion was celebrated. Melchizidek confirmed that it was the hand of the Lord that procured the victory for

Abraham (what would have happened if Abraham never attacked his enemy?). Finally, Abraham set forth the example of tithing by giving Melchizidek one tenth of all he had.

Abraham, Father of Faith

Jewish and Christian tradition teaches that Abraham was the "Father of Faith." However his life contradicts most people's definition of "faith." Many people define faith as trusting the Lord to bring the promise to pass without the participation of the individual.

As it was with Lot we see that the "Father of Faith" believed that he should do everything in his God-given ability to care for and protect that which was entrusted to him. This also included his family. Abraham took action to participate with God in bringing forth the fulfillment of the promise given him.

In his homily on the Scripture where Jesus said for the believer to let our requests be known to God, Chrysostom poses a rhetorical question. Since God knows all things then why does he require us to ask for what we need? He goes on to explain that God wants us to be a partner with him in life and not a spectator (Homily nineteen on Matthew).

The three young men, Abraham and countless other men and women of God put their lives and possessions in jeopardy to procure spiritual freedom. In the same way did the Founding Fathers commit their lives and fortunes to procure deliverance from the tyranny of the King of England. We who are the contemporaries of the Founding Fathers and the Fathers of Faith have a responsibility to procure liberty and freedom for ourselves and our posterity. To defend against those forces in society and government which would have the nation bow its' knee to the "golden image" which supplants the worship of God.

The tyranny we face today originates in the spiritual realm manisfesting in the natural, which is not content with coexisting with moral righteousness and economic responsibility, it seeks to totally eradicate it from public life.

In his book *"The Plan,"* Pat Robertson shares his experience in 1981 when he, *"truly realized the enormity of the plan of the ACLU, the N.E.A. and Planned Parenthood to destroy Christian values in America..."*

Human Effort-God's Blessing

In pondering the two biblical accounts of Abraham's deliverance of Lot and David's Psalm 149: 6-9, I am reminded of an experience I had several years ago as I was studying the Bible.

During that time the Lord gave me a "word of wisdom." In essence He said that when I am doing anything that is according to His perfect will and I use all my efforts, He will respond in the supernatural.

This promise was important because I was involved with my family's investments and real estate holdings. Soon I would be experiencing the manifestation of such a promise.

A short time later our family had an office building for lease. An offer was submitted to lease one third of the building. I was about to accept it when another company of great financial wealth said they wanted to lease the entire building. The hitch was that he had to get approval. This would take about two weeks. I was faced with the age old question of whether to take the bird in the hand or wait for the two birds in the bush.

I had asked the company who wanted the whole building what the chances were of getting the lease approved. He said: "I have never lost one yet."

After much prayer and hard work, I told my realtor that I was going to wait the two weeks and hope that the company desiring to lease the entire building would be able to get the lease approved.

Immediately after hanging up the telephone I lost the peace of God. I then had to discern whether I was experiencing an emotional disturbance or was this in fact a move of God's Spirit telling me that I had made a mistake.

About two hours went by until I decided that the lack of "peace" I was experiencing was, in fact, the Lord negatively responding to my decision. I then called my realtor to tell him that I changed my mind. He was not there and so I left a message for him to call me back.

An hour later he returned my call. When I told him that I changed my mind, he said in a bewildered way, "speak about the hand of God!"

When I asked him what he meant by that he explained that after I told him of my initial decision he called the other client to tell him I rejected his offer to lease the one third space. However, that client was not in the office. He then left the office and the client returned his call. Shortly thereafter I placed my call and left my message asking for a return call.

In conclusion, he just returned to the office and saw one message from me and one message from the other client. Naturally, he said, "I thought to call you first." I informed him of my change of mind.

About a year later I saw the client who had wanted to lease the entire building and after visiting for a while I was curious to know if he had ever gotten the approval. He said "no." Thank God for the Lord who responds in the supernatural when we put forth our maximum efforts in the natural.

So it will be in governmental affairs regarding the Body of Christ. If we imitate the actions of Abraham and David by using our natural abilities and resources coupled with worship and prayer, I am convinced that the Lord will respond in the supernatural way to honor our labors the same way He honored Abraham. Then we will be able to re-establish moral standards in public policy.

We are called upon to use our best efforts and hard work. God expects each of His people to use the analytical faculties of their mind to determine the actions to take. A man who has a wife and children does not need to "feel led" by the Lord to work in order to support the family. He already knows his responsibilities.

A Christian who takes their faith seriously will naturally be led to involvement within the political realm. As to what degree this involvement takes is dependent upon the individual's personal conviction and walk with the Lord but we are all required to get involved.

10

Queen Esther Did Not Want to Get Involved

In the Old Testament Book of Esther the Scripture focused on the relationship between the Jews, Ahasuerus, king of an empire that expanded from India to Ethiopia, Haman the king's chief counselor, and Mordecai a man of God. Mordecai was a man who would not compromise his faith and reverence to God and Esther, Queen of Ahasuerus.

Haman hated the Jews to the point of attempting to deceive the king Ahasuerus into issuing a decree to execute them. Mordecai (who was, in fact, Queen Esther's uncle) told Esther what Haman had done and that the king agreed to the genocide.

Mordecai told Esther that she needed to go before the king, draw upon her favor with him and her position as Queen to make supplication for the Jews.

Esther's response was self-serving, in light of the greater consequences. She told Mordecai that the person who comes before the king without being called by him will be executed except if the king extends his scepter to them.

Esther was afraid to use her political influence to effect the greatest good for the greatest number of people, the Jews and the inhabitants of the empire of Ahasuerus. The reason I include the inhabitants of all the empire is that they, being in subjection to Ahasuerus, will likewise experience the repercussions of God's judgment against the ruler who sought to destroy the inheritance of Abraham.

"And I will make of thee a great nation,
and I will bless thee, and make thy name
great; and thou shalt be a blessing: And
I will bless them that bless thee, and
curse him that curseth thee..." Genesis 2:2,3.

Mordecai's response to her is one which all Christian's today need to pay close attention:

"Then Mordecai commanded to answer Esther,
Think not with thyself that thou shall escape in
the king's house, more than all the Jews...
For if thou altogether holdest thy peace at this
time, then shall...deliverance arise to the Jews
from another place; but you and your father's
house shall be destroyed; and who knoweth
whether you are come to the kingdom for such
a time as this?" Esther 4:13.

Mordecai made clear that if she didn't approach the king she would assuredly be put to death. The delusion that she could escape this catastrophe was removed.

Esther was comfortable in her royalty. She was fearful for her life. Thus, she did not want to pursue approaching the king for fear of loosing both. So it is today. Many people do not want to exercise their rights of citizenship in the political process because they are comfortable in their living. They are fearful of being exposed to the potential adverse reaction from those of the political opposition. Many times Christians are fearful of being rejected, persecuted or ridiculed for their political and moral beliefs.

Mordecai, a man of deep commitment and trust in the Lord would not accept her reasons for not approaching the king but in fact brought the reality of the truth to Queen Esther's attention. Such reality was that her royalty and comfort would not protect her from the executioner's sword.

Esther awakened to this reality. Upon the King's command to destroy all the Jews, Esther's security would vanish. She saw clearly how that the hand of the Lord set her in the position of influence at the strategic moment.

Queen Esther Implements Spiritual and Natural Strategies

What happens next is highly crucial in understanding the application of political involvement from a Christian perspective. Esther implements two parallel strategies. One in the natural realm and one in the spiritual.

"Then Esther bade them return Moredecai this answer,
Go gather together all the Jews that are present in Shushan,
and fast ye for me, and neither eat nor drink three days,
night or day; I also and my maidens will fast likewise..." Esther 4:16.

Here we see the spiritual strategy. It is advisable to remember that no matter how great a plan a person has in the natural realm it will not succeed unless it is committed to the Lord in prayer and many times with fasting:

"Commit your works unto the Lord and your thoughts will be established" Proverbs 16:3.
"Except the Lord build the house, they labour in vain that build it; except the Lord keep the city, the watchman waketh but in vain" Psalm 127:1.

Esther, had made a conscious decision to totally commit herself and the success of her plans to the hand of God.

"...and so will I go in unto the king, which is not according to the law; if I perish, I perish" Esther 4:16.

The natural strategy was to apply all the God given skills, wisdom and knowledge that Esther had at her disposal. Three days after they began to fast and pray Esther put on her royal robes. These robes represent two important factors. First the robes represented the authority and position in the kingdom. She took hold of her position as queen. Secondly, the royal robes represented respect for the king Ahasuerus. These are the two key elements to success in the world. First, know our abilities and authority, and second be respectful of those in authority.

The Scriptures record that when Ahasuerus saw Esther immediately she had favor in his eyes. How could she have favor? She was an honorable woman who honored and loved her husband the king.

This can be seen by the way she approached the king. She went to the inner court and waited for the king's response.

When he offered her the scepter then she came near to him, evidencing her respect and honor for her king and husband. I say this because the king's previous wife, Vashti, was disobedient and disrespectful to him. Consequently he rejected her from being queen (Esther 1:19-2:1).

Secondly, and most important, favor of God and the favor of the king was with her. I believe that we can see this in the way the king spoke to her upon knowing that she had a request.

> *"Then said the king unto her, what wilt thou, queen Esther? and what is thy request? it shall be even given thee to the half of the kingdom"* Esther 5:3.

Esther exposes Haman and his maniacal plan against the Jews and in effect against the king himself. This resulted in the successful deposing of Haman and the safety of the Jews and the empire. This all occurred because the man of God (Mordecai) spoke to the queen and the queen acted upon her authority and the relationship she had with her husband having faithfully served and loved him.

Now we must take special note that even after Haman's plan the king did not unilaterally provide for the protection of the Jews from their enemies. Rather he issued a decree through Mordecai. A decree that would allow the Jews to gather and arm themselves for their protection (Esther 8:7-11).

Even though the plot against the Jews was exposed and the primary perpetrator was eliminated the king only provided the means for the Jews to protect themselves by giving the decree by his signet. The Jews had to act upon the authority given by the king through Mordecai.

I find it interesting that Haman was not killed either super naturally nor by natural causes but rather through the same governmental instrument of power that he sought to use to execute the man of God (Mordecai). This instance reminds me of a promise in the Book of Proverbs 11:8:

*"The righteous is delivered out of trouble,
and the wicked cometh in his stead."*

Mordecai Always Faithful

You might find it of interest to know that before this situation with Haman arose, Mordecai was instrumental in exposing a plot to overthrow the king. As a result, the two perpetrators were executed but Mordecai was never acknowledged.

During the time just preceding Esther's exposure of Haman's plans, the king was awakened in the middle of the night (by the Lord) and was stirred to review the book of the records where he saw that nothing had been done for Mordecai's act of loyalty. Consequently, the king gave to Mordecai all the wealth and authority that was Haman's.

The king Ahasuerus was surrounded by "captive Jews." One was his queen and the other was his Prime Minister. Both of whom had proven to be loyal, honorable and dedicated subjects.

Nowhere in the book of Esther was there an overt reference to the move of God in the events of the Book. I see the Lord doing this so that we can see that His move in the affairs of mankind are through man and not apart from him as we can see when Mordecai said to Esther:

*"...who knoweth whether thou art come
to the kingdom for such a time as this?"* Esther 4:14.

One of the great lessons that we can draw from this Book of Scripture regarding Christian involvement in government and politics is that for righteousness, mercy and prosperity to come to a nation, the wicked must be taken out of positions of authority. People (whether Christian or not) who adhere to the Judeo-Christian ethic need to take their place.

"Mercy and truth preserve the king: and his throne is upholden by mercy" Proverbs 20:28.

"Take away the wicked from before the king, and his throne shall be established in righteousness" Proverbs 25:5.

The message of the Book of Esther can be effectively summarized in the last chapter:

"And the king Ahasuerus laid a tribute upon the land, and upon the isles of the sea. And all the acts of his power and of his might, and the declaration of the greatness of Mordecai, whereunto the king advanced (made him great), are they not written of the kings of Media and Persia? For Mordecai the Jew was next unto the king Ahasuerus and great among the Jews and accepted of the multitude of his brethren, seeking the wealth of his people, and speaking peace to all his seed" Esther chapter ten.

This last chapter records that the king in his "power and might" demonstrated the subsequent prosperity and success of the king after he came to the defense of the Jews and by association the God of the Jews. Likewise I believe that America will grow in greatness, economically, morally, intellectually and militarily when she realigns her policies and actions with those of God as defined in the Judeo-Christian ethic.

This chapter also makes special note of Mordecai's religious affiliation *"For Mordecai the Jew..."* This tells us that in the greatness of his authority and honor given him by the king he never forgot his God or his people. The Scripture records that Moredecai was "next to the king Ahasuerus" in power and authority. How did he get there? He honored the king by revealing the death threat and he honored the Jews (the apple of God's eye) by revealing the death plot of Haman to destroy them.

Note that Mordecai did not simply "pray." He prayed and did all that he knew to do and God granted the favor to Esther to speak to the king. Who put him there? It was the Lord who moved upon the king when he couldn't sleep until he looked into the books to find that Mordecai had not been rewarded. Subsequently, Mordecai used his influence to bring wealth, peace and prosperity.

Lessons Of Esther

King Ahasuerus was an honorable king and sensitive to the love of his wife. It was his chief counselor, the wicked Haman, that lied to him. After the devious plan was exposed by Esther he became enraged and corrected the problem. Active involvement by the woman of God preserved the king, the kingdom, the Jews, and expelled evil.

Mordecai, the virtual prophet of the Lord started the process which led to Haman's death and the blessing of the Jews by an act of political protest when he refused to bow before Haman.

Haman, upset at Mordecai's visible resistance, devised the plan to destroy all of the Jews. The Results? Wicked Haman died, Mordecai was promoted and the Jews prospered. Think of it, all this because Moredecai staged a political protest.

When Esther heard about the impending destruction of the whole Jewish nation she sought to protect her own life by not getting involved. It is important for all Christians to hear the response of Mordecai:

> *"For if thou altogether holdest thy peace at this time,*
> *then shall their enlargement and deliverance*
> *arise to the Jews from another place: but thou and*
> *thy father's house shall be destroyed..."* Esther 4:14.

No matter what she would do, the deliverance of the Jews would be sent. This alternate deliverance would not save Esther and her family.

The same office of authority used by Haman to bring evil upon the Jews was also used by Mordecai to bring wealth and prosperity to them.

If Esther had not taken action she and her family would have been destroyed. What do you think will happen to Christians who, by not exercising their political rights as citizens, allow the power of government into the hands of those who do not adhere to sound moral policies?

We may want to remember that the cancer that kills a person starts with only a small cell in the body. Then left untreated, it grows until the situation becomes terminal. The Apostle Paul addresses this principle when he says that a little leaven leavens the whole lump (I Corinthians 5:6,7).

As we can see, the governmental office of authority and power is virtually amoral. Rather it is like a car, electricity or other vehicle. In the hands of immoral people the power of the office will effect immorality upon the nation. Likewise, when those positions of authority are occupied by people who are established in the moral traditions of the Judeo-Christian ethic the authority of the governmental office will be used to establish righteousness in the land and that nation will receive the blessings of God.

So it will be for the Christian community who will or will not use their civic rights and abilities to effect righteousness for the nation. Deliverance will come from another way but judgment will come upon those who say or do nothing.

This is an amazing parallel to the story of Joseph who helped Pharoah protect against the seven years of famine by interpreting his dream and consequently Pharaoh was able to prepare for its coming. Joseph, as with Mordecai, was made the second most powerful man in the kingdom.

When God established the events in the cases of Mordecai and Joseph He was establishing a precedent for us today in 20th century America. Namely, that prayer and action moves God's hand of deliverance and blessing.

If Christians will hold to the lessons given to us by the Book of Esther (Moses, David, Joseph, et al) we too could see our government leaders surrounded by godly, loyal and honorable people. For such an event to occur there only need to be prayer and corresponding action to elect these people and pass laws which stand upon the foundation of the Judeo-Christian ethic.

Corresponding Action to Prayer

There are two different categories of political involvement. The first is "active." This would include running for office, working as an aide to a candidate, volunteer supporter in the campaign doing such things as making telephone calls, walking door to door, passing out campaign literature, etc.

The second category of political involvement could be described as "passive." This type of involvement would include doing such things as writing letters to the editor and government/civic leaders. Being prepared to intelligently discuss issues with family, friends and neighbors. Attend meetings to support your position. Last, to be sure to vote.

In either case it is important for each person to determine for themselves what God would have them do. As there are many offices of ministry in the Church they are all important. The Ministry of Helps has the same importance to God as the ministry of the Evangelist. Each has their "calling" and responsibility. So it is with political activity. Some people will be led of the Lord to run for office and others to address envelopes for a candidate.

The important key is that each person take action to bring forth sound government and laws to the Land that honor God and bless the nation.

Therefore God's formula for success is a simple one... "Our labor—His favor."

11

Judges
God's People—God's Deliverers

The theme of the Book of Judges shows that Israel was a rebellious nation. This led to captivity under oppressive nations. When Israel repented the Lord effected their freedom by the hand of Deliverers also known as Judges.

Most of the time these people were simple and unassuming. However, when the Spirit of the Lord came upon them, they became mighty Deliverers for God.

This can be seen in the lives of people like Gideon. His life illustrates the hand of God making weak people great and the necessity to fulfill the responsibility of leadership.

In the Book of Judges, we see how Israel experienced this. *"...the children of Israel did evil in the sight of the Lord and the Lord delivered them into the hand of Midian for seven years"* Judges 6:1.

When they cried out to the Lord for deliverance an angel was sent to Gideon at a time when he was gathering wheat. It is important to note this because Gideon was shown to be a man of hard work and diligence.

The angel called him a "mighty man of valor" through whom God was to deliver Israel. Gideon's humility came forth in his response by saying he was "poor" and the "least (youngest)" in his father's house. Obviously, God loves to use the weak things of the world to confound the things that are mighty. (1 Corinthians 1:27).

When the angel of the Lord gave the word to Gideon that he was chosen to set Israel free Gideon out of a sincere heart tested the word of the angel. Upon knowing that the word was true he made a covenant with God to fulfill the task. Gideon listened to God, obeyed him and procured the victory.

An interesting observation to make is that he was not a man of war but a grain farmer. Yet, when he said yes to God, the Spirit of the Lord endowed him with wisdom and power to be what he was not. Such is the effectiveness of God's people when they release themselves in faith to the will and wisdom of God.

The time period covered by the Book establishes a pattern of God's plan for the personal involvement in public affairs by His people. He is also demonstrating that no matter how far into sin His people fell He was always ready to deliver them if they would repent.

Invariably God's deliverance came through the hand of people the world saw as weak and incapable. People like Gideon who was called by God to deliver Israel even though he was not a soldier and believed himself incapable. Through God's strength and their labors Israel was set free.

When Gideon and his men defeated the Midianites, the people wanted him to be king. However, Gideon would not accept their request. It seems he was refusing God's call to leadership over the nation.

Gideon wanted God to rule over Israel. Though his intentions were honorable he did not understand that God had irrevocably established the monarchy over Israel. The prophetic word God gave to David that his seed would rule over Israel testifies to this. (Psalm 132:11, 12) God desired to rule over Israel through the hand of man as He had done historically.

After all, the nation of Israel had requested that they be ruled by a king and not by Theocracy. That is why the Prophet Samuel anointed Saul to be king in the first place.

When God responded to the desire of Israel to be ruled by a king. God established the monarchy. It was never His will for that monarchy (government) to be divorced from the moral and spiritual standards that God established.

What Gideon did not see was that without the man of God on the throne, Israel would depart from the Lord, to be given into the hand of her enemies. He was sincere in his rejection of being king but he was sincerely wrong. So it is with many Christians today. They want God to influence government to change public policy but they do not want to be the ones through whom He would effect the change.

The consequences in both events will be the same. The nation's policies lead to oppression under their enemies. For Israel her oppressors were the other surrounding nations. For America her oppressors are illiteracy, crime, violence, immorality, and bankrupt fiscal policies.

Gideon's rejection to fulfill the call of God resulted in a power void. Subsequently, his son Abimalek became king. The consequences were disastrous.

First, Abimalek surrounded himself with incompetent men who the Scriptures call "...vain and light persons..." (Judges 9:4) This is a great deal different than what his father did when he took thirty thousand men and reduced them to just 300 who were cunning, sharp and committed to the mission.

Abimalek then did the unthinkable. He set out to kill seventy of his brothers. Finally, he himself was killed by the men of Shechem. For this the men of Shechem were cursed by God,

The deaths of all his sons and the curse on the men of Shechem could have been avoided if Gideon understood that it was God's plan for him to rule over Israel. Gideon started the work of Israel's deliverance. However, he did not complete it. He availed himself to conquer her physical enemy but not to lead them in the ways of righteousness and truth in the worship of the God of their Fathers.

Those who love God need to understand that His great hand of deliverance is through His people. In the days of Gideon, the instrument of deliverance was the sword. For America today, we have a two edged sword. The ballot box and government authority. This is the "sword" through which we can be protected by moral domestic and foreign policies. The second edge of the sword is the strength of our armed forces to protect us from external enemies. In both cases the sword must be taken by the hand of those who adhere to sound judgment and skill in its use.

As Israel needed to be delivered through the acts of man empowered by God so it is today for America. Faith and prayer must be accompanied by thoughtful, prayerful works of labor in the fields of political involvement in all levels of government and civic affairs.

Let us recall that the great civil rights movement of the 1960's started in a small Baptist Church by a relatively unknown Baptist minister motivated by his moral convictions. His name was Dr. Martin Luther King. His voice called for justice, peace and reconciliation.

Because Dr. King moved upon his Christian convictions he brought about the most sweeping social change in American history and did it in a peaceful, legal and legislative manner setting an example for millions in the world today. All because a Christian minister took his faith seriously and applied it in the public affairs of society and government. In recent years we are beginning to see this involvement accelerate.

In the Congressional elections of 1994, according to polling data from the Christian Coalition, nearly thirty three per cent of voters were born again Christians or pro family Roman Catholics. While this may give the appearance of wide range Christian participation in politics it is rather very small when viewed in the context of all Christians of voting age in the United States. The trend is going in the right direction but there's a long way to go.

Some people are oblivious to the moral issues of the day because they are under the delusion that other peoples' immoral behavior does not affect them. They are wrong. For example, many believe that A.I.D.S affects mainly homosexuals and drug users. The truth is that the government is spending billions of dollars on research to find a cure. Instead of stopping the behavior that spreads the disease special interest groups lobby government to spend more. Where do those billions of dollars come from? All of us tax payers.

These billions of dollars do not take into consideration the tremendous health care costs paid by hospitals and insurance companies to care for those afflicted with the disease. Who pays for it? You guessed right again, the American taxpayers, insurance companies (the Americans who pay insurance premiums reflect these costs).

So it is with increased crime. If we are not a direct victim we are an indirect one. For example, credit card fraud and other types crime, cause increased insurance claims by the client who loses the money. These costs are passed on to us the consuming public.

There is much to learn from the mistakes and victories of Israel. When righteous men lead the nation there will be peace and prosperity in the land and deliverance from her enemies. When righteousness departed from the life governance of the king the nation fell into sin. The consequences that followed were God's judgment of death, destruction or bondage.

When America cast God out from the public schools she came out from under the "wings" of His protection. Moral absolutes were undermined. Anxiety, stress, crime and violence, moral decay and debauchery have replaced sound morality as the pillars of society. Instead of teaching the Bible precepts of chastity until marriage as the only "safe sex," condoms are being given under the guise that they provide "safer sex."

Many in America, including the Judicial Courts believed that America's greatness was derived from herself. This was seen in a decision of the U.S. Court of Appeals for the ninth circuit on March 6, 1996 which struck down a Washington State ban on doctor assisted suicide. The opinion stated that "competent, terminally ill patients" have a constitutional right to choose "the time and manner" of their own death. Thus, this court has effectively negated the role of God as the benefactor of human life and putting man in His place in determining issues of life and death. Consequently this philosophy also makes it more convenient to expel God from other areas of public life.

As it was with the nation of Israel so is it with America who has known God's love, mercy and prosperity. God is looking for men and women who will hear and answer His call to lead the nation on the path of righteousness that "...Shines brighter and brighter unto the noonday sun" (Proverbs 4:18).

God's intent is for America to live in peace, safety and prosperity. However, this can happen only when she lives according to the standards set by the Benefactor of peace, safety and prosperity.

When one goes outside on a rainy day he can expect to feel the rain. When America departs from the House of God's precepts and laws, she can expect to feel the pain. Will we who possess the keys to God's protection, peace and life open the door for America to come back home?

12

Civil Affairs in the New Testament

Although the primary focus of the New Testament was on the spiritual life of mankind we can see many supportive references to Christian participation in civic and government affairs. Many were spoken by Jesus Himself as well as the Apostles and John the Baptist.

The Scriptures do not specifically address the subject of Christian involvement in civic affairs. The reason? God was laying the foundation of life. First the salvation of the soul. Second the manifestation of the believer's new life reflected in society.

A good example of this can be seen through Paul's letter to Philemon, a prominent Christian whose slave Onesiumus had run away and joined Paul. Paul's letter to Philemon was intended to bring reconciliation, mercy and justice to both parties.

Paul addressed the issue of slavery by addressing the heart of it. Onesimus would be a better laborer and Philemon would not look at him as a slave, but a brother in the Lord who was in his employ.

In "Christianizing" society, slavery would ultimately be rejected as an institution delivering the person and nation from this philosophy of bondage. This happened when slavery was abolished through the acts of government provoked by the conscience of people such as the abolitionists applying their Christian principles by standing against it.

The New Testament establishes a three tier approach to mankind and life on earth which are separate, *but related*. First, we see Jesus addressing the spiritual needs of mankind. Namely, man's separation from God, the fallen nature, death and God's holy remedy. Secondly, personal relationships between God and man are addressed by the Lord through His parables and teachings. Third, we see the interrelationship between man and government or should I say "those in authority." The exception to extending obedience to them is if their policies and edicts are contrary to the Christian faith. For example, Christians were expected to pay taxes but they were required to reject the order to offer incense in worship of Caesar.

Caesar Augustus

Throughout the Old Testament we saw examples of God's sovereignty in the affairs of the kingdoms of man. In the New Testament, God demonstrates that He continues His reign.

In Luke 2:1-7 we read that Caesar Augustus issued the decree that all peoples should go back to their hometown for the recording of the census. This resulted in Mary and Joseph going to Bethlehem where Jesus was to be born, thereby fulfilling the prophetic Scripture of Micah 5:2 which foretells that the Messiah will come from Bethlehem.

Thus, we see that the hand of God moved in the government of men to bring forth His divine plan. Even now we can see the divine wisdom of God in this act of sovereign power. The Romans were pagans who did not know the Hebrew God, they did not even believe He existed, and would not obey Him. After all, He was the God of those they conquered.

However, God moved the whole empire just to bring the expectant Mary and Joseph to Bethlehem. The Lord could have spoken to Joseph in a dream the same way He confirmed that the baby in Mary's womb was the divine Son of God. Or, as He did when he warned Joseph to take the child to Egypt to escape Herod's butchery.

What was God's reason for moving the entire empire? There are two primary ones. The first is rooted in a personal application of divine wisdom and hope to all believers. In this act of sovereign power we see God moving an entire empire to fulfill one prophesy to the least of the Princes of Judah (Micah 5:2) i.e. Bethlehem. How much more would he move heaven and earth to fulfill one promise to those for whom He died?

The second is a contemporary reason. God, knowing all things from eternity to eternity, established His continued reign in the affairs of man. Therefore, involvement by His people in government is an integral part of His perfect will.

The First Miracle: Water Into Wine

Jesus' first miracle was the changing of the water into wine. Why did Jesus choose this miracle to launch His ministry? John

Chrysostom says that Jesus did this in order to demonstrate that He came to fulfill man's material and spiritual needs. Here again we see the confluence of the spiritual and earthly kingdoms; man's relative needs in both and God's intent to fulfill those needs equally.

Duty of Citizenship

"Render unto Caesar the things that belong to Caesar and to God the things that belong to God" Luke 20:25.

This Scripture records when the chief priests were trying to trick Jesus into rebellion against the state so as to have some excuse to accuse Him of wrong doing.

The fact that Jesus distinguishes those things that *"belong to Caesar"* and those things that *"belong to God"* does not mean that the two are mutually exclusive, for we know that God owns all things and possesses all things.

The motivation for Jesus to make such a seemingly dichotomous statement is to reveal the mind of God concerning civic and spiritual responsibilities. Both are necessary and in God's perfect will.

In Matthew 17:27 Jesus declares the necessity to pay the tribute to Caesar:

"...(Peter) go to the sea and cast a hook, and take up the first (fish) that comes up; and when you have opened his mouth, you shall find a piece of money: That take and give unto them for you and me."

Since Jesus and the Apostles had money (Judas was the treasurer John 12:3-6), we may want to ask: Why didn't Jesus tell Peter to get the money from the treasury? The answer can be seen in that Jesus wanted to teach us that His blessings come through the combination of our labor and His favor.

Peter was a fisherman and Jesus told him to go fishing. The supernatural blessing was that this fish was of more value than what was perceived for it had a coin in its mouth of such value that it paid all the tribute.

How does this relate to Christian involvement in civic affairs in the twentieth century? This story demonstrates that Jesus honors civic responsibilities. We are instructed to do as well. In the same manner Jesus will bless our efforts if we will cast in the "hook" of our labors into the sea of public affairs to fulfill our civic responsibilities.

God placed in America the governmental system where godly people can have an influence and moral righteousness can be the pillars of law and society. This can only be done if those people who adhere to the Judeo Christian ethic are diligent to be aware of their responsibilities and apply them.

The Office and Office Holder

When Jesus spoke to the Jews about the Pharisees he alluded to the dichotomy of the institutional office and the person who possesses the authority of its power.
> *"...the Scribes and Pharisees sit in Moses seat.*
> *All therefore they command you that do,*
> *for they say and do not"* Matthew 23:2, 3.

Jesus is helping the people understand the nature of authority vis a vi the integrity of those who possess its office. This can be seen in governmental affairs as well as religious ones. Herein we see the parallel between the spiritual and natural kingdoms.

We see this principle once again when Caiaphas, actually spoke this prophesy

> "...one man should die for the people and that the
> whole nation perish not. Caiaphas did not say this
> on his own. As high priest that year, he was
> prophesying that Jesus would die for the nation" John 11:50, 51.

The desire of Caiaphas was not to bring forth the word of God but rather to fulfill his sinister desire intended for Jesus. Caiaphas was admonishing the other Pharisees who were troubled about what to do with Jesus. He was ready to kill Jesus in hopes of preventing the Romans from taking away their place (nation).

However, God spoke through him because he sat in the "seat of the high priest". Therefore, even though he was evil in heart he was still in the office of authority which God established and through which He spoke.

Pontius Pilate the Hand of Roman Authority

When Jesus was taken by the Romans to go before Pilate it is advantageous for us to keep in mind that Pilate was the hand of the same Roman Empire that God used to fulfill the prophecy that the Messiah would be born in Bethlehem of Judea.

This is also the same empire that God will use to proclaim the innocence of Jesus.

> "Then said Pilate to the chief priests and to the
> people, I find no fault in this man" Luke 23:4.

> *"...You have brought this man to me as*
> *one that perverts the people and behold,*
> *I have examined him before you, have found*
> *no fault in this man touching those things*
> *which you accuse him: No, Nor yet Herod:*
> *for I sent you to him; and lo nothing worthy*
> *of death is done unto him"* Luke 23:14,15.

Herein we see the office of government used to exonerate Jesus from any wrongdoing. Therefore, as a matter of public record, any suffering inflicted upon him will be done to an innocent man and unjustified.

Pilate's problem came when he put himself in the vulnerable position of opening the door to punishing Jesus. Therefore, when he had Him scourged and crucified Pilate did so out of his own error in judgment contradicting his own findings. Therefore, he joins Judas in being guilty of sin. As Jesus said,

> *"You (Pilate) could have no power at all*
> *against me except it were given you from*
> *above: therefore he that delivered me to*
> *you has the greater sin"* John 19:11.

In this verse Jesus confirms that the power of the Roman Empire and Pilate's authority came from God. However, Pilate's improper use of that power is what caused him to sin.

Jesus Christ King of the Jews

> *"And Pilate wrote a title and put it on*
> *the cross. And the writing was, JESUS OF*
> *NAZARETH THE KING OF THE JEWS"* John 19:19.

This inscription was written in Greek, Hebrew and Latin. Why? Why not just one language? Why wasn't it written in Aramaic which was the language that Christ spoke? The answer can be found in understanding the role of all three languages in the region during those days in history.

Greek was the social language of the empire. Hebrew was the religious/ethnic language of the Jews. Latin was the language of the Roman government.

Therefore, God was using the institution of government to proclaim the Lordship of Jesus in all matters of social, religious and governmental matters of life. Thus, revealing the broad range of Christ's dominion and influence in the affairs of mankind.

Ananias the High Priest

Once again we see the divinely appointed office of the High Priest being corrupted and abused by those who sought their own glory and not that which comes from God.

Paul affirms respect for the office even though the office holder was corrupt, self serving, and resistant to the gospel message:

> *"And the high priest Ananias commanded them that stood by him to smite him on the mouth. Then said Paul unto him, God shall smite thee, thou whited wall; for sittest thou to judge me after the law, and commandest me to be smitten contrary to the law?..."*
> *"And they that stood by said, do you revile God's high priest? Then said Paul, I did not know, brethren that he was the high priest, for it is written, thou shalt not speak evil of the ruler of thy people"* Acts 23:2-5.

Therefore, Paul reaffirms the principle that when evil is perpetrated through the office of authority it is through the corruption of the office holder and not the institution of the office itself.

John The Baptist

Through the life of John the Baptist whom Jesus calls the greatest of all the prophets we can gain a great understanding of the positive affects on people when those office holders administer their responsibilities with righteousness.

John's first statement regarding the position of the government office came when he reproved Herod the Tetrarch for his immoral behavior. By publicly reproving Herod, John was holding this government official to an even higher level of accountability. Why? Because he is in the office of leadership and his immorality sets the standard for the moral behavior of the nation.

The Apostle Paul applies this same method of response to the leadership in the Church as he articulated in I Timothy 5:19,20.

> *"Against an elder receive not an accusation,*
> *but before two or three witnesses. Them that*
> *sin rebuke before all, that others also may fear."*

John the Baptist was severely and publicly reproving Herod for two additional reason. The first was to deal with his sin as it affects Herod's personal and professional life. Secondly, he was setting the tone for national repentance in preparation for the advent of the Messiah.

John The Baptist, The Soldiers and Publicans

John the Baptist in a unique manner speaks to the validity
of government service and Christian values.

> *"Then came also Publicans to be baptized,*
> *and said unto him, Master, what shall we do?*
> *And he said unto them. Exact no more than*
> *that which is appointed you.*

> *And the Solders likewise demanded of him,*
> *saying, and what shall we do? And he said*
> *unto them, do no violence to no man, neither*
> *accuse any falsely, and be content with your*
> *wages"* Luke 3:12-14.

John could have instructed them to stop their involvement
in government affairs and follow him. We might recall that these
two offices were scorned by the Jews because the Publicans
were exacting more taxes than what they should and the soldiers were the "hand" of Roman Tyranny.

Nevertheless, John did not require them to forsake their
offices. In fact the contrary is true. He told them how to properly carry out their duties with honesty and integrity.

He told the Publican to collect only the correct amount of
tax. The soldiers were told not to be violent to people by abus-
ing their power. He also said to be content with their wages so
as to not be vulnerable to corruption.

Consequently, John was telling them to go back to their
offices of government authority and service, applying the righ-

teousness they had received through repentance and baptism. Thereby beccomming true public servants through proper use of the authority that God had established.

The key element to understanding this encounter in regard to Christian involvement in government is to reference Matthew 3:4:

> *"And the same John had his raiment of camel's*
> *hair, and a leathern girdle about his loins;*
> *and his meat was locusts and wild honey."*

This Scripture identifies John, more than any other prophet, as one who repudiated worldliness that leads away from God. Therefore, if John was rejecting the governmental institutions in addition to the "fallen nature" of the world, surely he would discourage involvement in these institutions.

Cornelius—Luke 7:1-10

In this Scripture we see a Roman government official who showed respect, love and support for the Jewish faith and people. He used his political and governmental authority to help the Jews and their faith. Thus, when his servant was ill to the point of death, he asked the Jews to interecede with Jesus.

> *"And when they came to Jesus, they asked*
> *Him instantly, saying that he was worthy*
> *for whom He should do this: For he loves our*
> *nation and he has built us a synagogue"* Luke 7:4,5.

What?! Do we see money and influence of an anti-Jewish and an anti-God government being used to build a synagogue?

Absolutely! What does Jesus say about this relationship between "Church and state?"

"Jesus went with them..." Luke 7:6.

Thus, by a simple act of compliance, Jesus endorsed the Centurion's act of love and life of service to God through His authority in government. Jesus not only commended him for his faith, but he actually presented him to the people as a man who had greater faith than any in all of Israel. Thereby endorsing his faith and its application in government.

How did Cornelius understand the operation of faith? He answers this question himself when he paralleled the civic authority he had over his men to Jesus authority in the kingdom of the unseen. Thus, his civic authority in governmental office (as set up by God) helped him understand and receive faith in Jesus' power...just like God intends. Let's listen to the words of Cornelius the Roman Centurion:

"Wherefore neither thought I myself worthy
to come to you: but say in a word and my
servant shall be healed. For I also am a
man of authority, having under me soldiers,
and I say to one, go and goes; and to another,
Come and he comes; and to my servant, do this
and he does it. When Jesus heard these things
he marveled at him, and turned him about, and
said unto the people that followed him. I say
unto you, I have not found so great faith,
no, not in Israel" Luke 7: 7-9.

The consummation of Cornelius' acts was that his servant was saved from death, the Jews had their synagogue built and the Jews see that the kingdom of God will be made available to the Gentiles as prophesied by Isaiah.

What might have happened had Cornelius chosen not to enter the military? First, the Jews may well have been under a tyrant or at least one who did not care for them or God. After all the Jews were the conquered nation.

Secondly, we may have been deprived of such a faith-building and teaching example as seen through the life of the Centurion.

> *"When Jesus heard these things he marveled at him, and turned him about, and said unto the people that followed him. I say unto you, I have not found so great faith, no, not in Israel."*

Third, this Centurion may not have encountered the Messiah, the Fountainhead of life and received the gift of Christ's word for his servant and personal life.

Finally, we would not be able to see the profound benefits of a righteous man involved in human government using his authority to serve God and man.

Cornelius—Acts Chapter Ten

There is another Cornelius who was a Centurion in the Roman Army. Very possibly this was the same man spoken of in Luke chapter seven. Both of these men were close to their servants, honorable righteous and sincere before God.

Unlike the first encounter when the Centurion sought out Jesus this man's prayers and good works of charity entreated the Lord. Consequently, God sent His angel to show him the way to the fullness of the relationship with God.

Upon hearing the testimony of Cornelius, Peter's words in Acts 10:2,35 confirm that he was a man that feared God and worked righteousness in the execution of his responsibilities to the Emperor and the people.

This Centurion neither had the born again experience nor did he have the Baptism in the Holy Spirit and yet this was a man who was *a "devout man, and one that feared God with all his house..."*

He was able to successfully combine his responsibilities to the state with his faith and fear in God being loyal to both. This man was not even a Jew and he fulfilled both responsibilities admirably.

If he accomplished such great deeds with his faith, how much greater can be the believer's accomplishments seeing we have access to the mind of Christ, the Head of all authority.

The Ethiopian Eunuch

One of the greatest testaments to the positive influence that Christians can have when occupying the seat of government is seen in the story of the Ethiopian Eunuch.

He was a man of great honor. We know this because he was entrusted with the riches of Queen Candice.

He was sincerely seeking the love and righteousness of the Hebrew God. This can be seen in that he possessed his own copy of the Scripture. Remember, they did not have xerox machines to duplicate the Bible.

Phillip found him reading the Scriptures while standing in his chariot and not sitting in a synagogue where one would be expected to be found reading the Scriptures.

The greatness of his authority was paralleled by his great humility. This was demonstrated when he, first, asked Phillip, a total stranger, for the understanding of the Scripture he was reading. Secondly, when he was willing to be baptized by Phillip in a water hole.

As I think of this I am reminded of Naman the Syrian who had leprosy. When the prophet of God told him to dip seven times in the river, he became proud and indignant.(II Kings 5:9-11) The Ethiopian Eunuch, on the other hand, was able to see the wisdom of such an act through the eyes of humility.

This man's contrast of humility and great authority further establishes the wondrous possibilities for those who love God and are effective administrators.

The Eunuch's conversion was not held to himself but he effectively blended "religion" and "politics." How? As we can see, the whole Ethiopian nation was converted to Christ and even today the people from Ethiopia are Orthodox Christians who trace their faith back to the Ethiopian Eunuch. This nation lived in peace for centuries and overcame invasion from the Italians in World War II using little more than pitchforks and farm tools.

Chrysostom makes an interesting observation that unlike Cornelius in Acts chapter ten, this man was not referred to by name but only by his position in government and his relation to God.

He goes on to say that the Eunuch possessed four unique attributes which teaches us the key to political and spiritual success in the administration of one's life and the affairs of government.

The Eunuch: Moral purity in his personal life. Great authority: Diligent and wise to administer the authority that is given no matter how great or small. Authority over the Treasury: Integrity and honesty in busi-

ness dealings. Committed to worship God: Sets one's standards of excellence to higher levels of accountability.

When I enter into an Orthodox Church and see Ethiopian believers I ponder in amazement that their faith is rooted from a single man who was great and humble.

The life of the Ethiopian Eunuch testifies of the impact one righteous person in high government office can have upon a nation for generations.

Herod

A dramatic example of heavenly involvement in human government occurred in Acts 12:1-24. This Scripture relates the story of King Herod who was about to speak to the people of Tyre.

Because of certain events Herod was angered at the people. The people there were very concerned because they drew much prosperity from the king's country.

Hoping to incur his favor (and be politically correct) the people, upon hearing his oration, proclaimed him to be a god and not a man. Then, because he did not give glory to God the angel of the lord struck him with worms.

*"And upon a set day Herod, arrayed in
royal apparel, sat upon his throne, and
made an oration unto them...
And the people gave a shout saying, It
is the voice of a god, and not of a man...
And immediately the angel of the Lord
smote him, because he gave not God the
glory: and he was eaten of worms, and
gave up the ghost...But the word
of God grew and multiplied..."Acts 12:1-24.*

One might say that if God wanted His people to be involved in the government why didn't He have one of His people attack Herod instead of an angel?

The answer to this is multifold. The first is that if a Christian attacked Herod there would be an immediate and violent reaction against all Christians, branding them as traitors and that may well have hindered the spread of the gospel.

Second, it would confuse the believers who were told to give honor to the king and to "render unto Caesar that which is Caesar's."

Third, by Herod being struck with worms while he was arrayed in his royal apparel we can understand that God is God and He reigns in earthly and heavenly affairs. Herod abused his governmental responsibilities and thought of himself more than he should because he did not give God the glory.

Fourth, the people of Tyre and Sidon then saw that, as the Book of Proverbs says,

> *"many seek the ruler's favor but every mans'*
> *judgment comes from God"* Proverbs 29:26.

They viewed Herod as their "source" but in reality God is the fountainhead of all power and prosperity.

Kingdom Of God On Earth

While God desires for His children to be involved in civic and governmental affairs we need remember that the true and eternal kingdom of God will arrive with the second coming of the Lord Jesus Christ. It may be considered that the government of men is a type of caretaker government until that great day.

In the meantime we are to use our gifts and abilities to build our society on the moral standards governing faith and conduct. The results of which bring forth life, prosperity and health for the nation.

Paul uses his political authority for the sake of the Gospel..."*I appeal to Caesar...*" Acts 25:11.

This was the famous statement by Paul applying his civil rights as a Roman Citizen. This commenced the long encounter between the government of Rome and Paul as he preached the gospel.

The application of his civil rights as a Roman Citizen brought him before high government officials, Roman guards and even to the house of Caesar himself.

This should answer any question whether Christians should utilize any and all civil authority to promote the gospel and defend the rights of all believers in America. Paul did not back away from the challenge to his civil rights but he stood strong.

"...Ministers of God..."

To better understand the mind of Christ concerning Christian involvement in politics we can look further into Romans 13:1-7,

> *"Let every soul be subject to the higher*
> *powers. For there is no power but of God;*
> *the powers that be are ordained of God...*
> *Whosoever therefore resists the power,*
> *resists the ordinance of God; and they*
> *that resist shall receive to themselves damnation...*
> *For rulers are not a terror to good works,*
> *but to the evil. Will you then not be afraid*
> *of the power? Do that which is good and you*

> *shall have praise of the same...*
> *For he is a minister of God to you for good.*
> *But if you do that which is evil, be afraid;*
> *for he bears not the sword in vain; for he*
> *is the minister of God, a revenger to execute*
> *wrath upon him that does evil...*
> *Wherefore you need to be subject not only for*
> *wrath, but also ; for they are God's ministers,*
> *attending continually upon this very thing...*
> *Render therefore to all their dues; tribute*
> *to whom tribute is due; custom to whom custom;*
> *fear to whom fear; honor to whom honor."*

We are first admonished to be subject to the higher powers. The higher powers, in this context, are the governmental authorities. Secondly, the sovereignty of God's authority reigns in governmental affairs. Third, all powers are ordained of God. This clearly articulates that government rule is in the perfect will of God designed to protect and bless mankind.

Warning is given not to resist the authority of government. This verse is speaking of general governmental authority which enforces such laws that protect life and liberty in accord with the biblical standards of truth. When governmental actions infringe upon any inalienable right as given by God then it is the duty of the citizenry to respond accordingly.

God established government authority. Does it stand to reason that He want's His people to have an interest in who occupies these offices of "ministry"?

During the fourth century, Ambrose of Milan once said that the maintenance of civil law is secondary to that of religious interests. He recognized that without the religious underpinnings of the code of moral law given by God, there will be no stability for the nation and that nation will run adrift.

Let us remember that it was in a Southern Baptist Church that Martin Luther King launched the Civil rights movement of the sixties. This also set the tone for peaceful demonstrations in attempting to change public policy for future generations.

The Spiritual and Natural

One day while jogging, I began to pray. When I looked up to the sky I saw a vision of angelic armies battling the armies of evil. I kept praying and then saw that the angels were soundly winning the battle.

I then stopped praying to watch the battle. Thereupon the angels seemed to begin retreating. I quickly began to pray and the angels regained their dominance in the battle.

When the vision was over I was deeply concerned at the appearance of God's angels losing to the forces of evil. I asked the Lord why the angels were retreating. He responded to me, *"My angels were not retreating. They were withdrawing."*

Then the Lord revealed to me that His release of power in the earth is directly related to the intercession of His people. It is the will of God to include His children into the divine plan and not to be a spectator to it.

I then remembered the words of Jesus:

> *"...All power is given unto me in heaven and in earth. Go and teach all nations..."* Matthew 28: 18,19.
> *"And the seventy returned again with joy, saying, Lord, even the devils are*

*subject unto us through thy name....And He
said unto them ...Behold I give unto you power
to tread on serpent and scorpions and over
all the power of the enemy"* Luke 10:17,18.

Separation of Church and State

Many ask how the "separation between Church and State" would be applied in the context of Christian involvement in politics. The answer is simple: It doesn't. There is no separation between church and state. He who created the one also created the other. Church and state came from God's own mouth. To attempt separating church and state is tantamount to attempting the separation between the body and soul. The end result of such separation is death. Since God created the church and state, then it is His intention to manifest his presence through both.

Imagine how many millions of children would be alive today if God-fearing people governed and judged according to the Judeo Christian ethic. How many less victims of crime would there be if biblical principles of personal responsibility were administered to criminals rather than making excuses for them?

God has provided the institution of Government, the wisdom of His written Word, His grace and the freedom to exercise our inalienable rights to benefit the nation and mankind. People of faith need to be people of action.

13

The Early Church

The Great Commission

"Go ye therefore, and teach all nations,
baptizing them in the name of the Father,
and of the Son and of the Holy Ghost:
Teaching them to observe all things
whatsoever I have commanded you: And lo
I am with you always even unto the end
of the world" Matthew 28:19, 20.

Just prior to His ascent into heaven Jesus spoke what became known as the Great Commission. This also became the foundation of the ministry of all Christendom.

The salvation message of The Great Commission also implies that we are to affect society, government and the economic state of nations. Not to establish a theocracy but to establish God's principles and statutes for mankind to live. In itself this would bear testimony to the validity of the Gospel of Jesus Christ.

Each individual, through their works and manner of life would be the "light" and "salt". Since government is an integral part of society it too would be influenced by the gospel. One may ask why should Christianity influence society and government? Isn't it a personal faith? The answer is simple: Christianity and the Judeo-Christian ethic has all the answers to life's questions and problems—providing a secure standard for living.

This will never happen if those who subscribe to His principles do not apply them in society and government. When the teachings of Jesus Christ are sincerely believed and received they manifest themselves in the natural world.

Cyril of Jerusalem said, *"The Church extends over the whole world. That is why it is called 'universal.' It brings the whole race of mankind, governors and the governed into subjection to godliness."*

The intention of Jesus' commission was to save souls and build society establishing government upon the foundation of His teachings. For the Gospel to affect people's lives and yet be kept from government and society is like trying to keep the sweet smell of a rose from going from one room to another. By its' nature it cannot be limited.

Advent of the Messiah

In setting the stage for the advent of the Messiah, God uses governments to prepare the way.

> *"But when the fullness of the time was come, God sent forth his son, made of a woman, made under the law"* Galatians 4:4.

What is this *"fullness of time"*? Church and world history show us that God had set in place various governments from Alexander the Great to the Roman Empire in order to prepare the way for the Messiah.

The conquests of Alexander brought a unity of language throughout the empire. Namely the Greek language which made communication of the message of Christ more effective. The Roman empire helped prepare the way of the ministry of the Church by establishing a worldwide travel network and a cohesive government which would provide protection for the travelers.

Therefore, when the Church was "birthed" at Pentecost the preparations had been made to facilitate the spread of the gospel. There was a unifying social language, strong government which provided the protection, communication and travel network.

Politics and the Early Church

Although there has been little expressly taught by the Early Church as to Christian involvement in government affairs, the Church tacitly approved of it. Some of the Church Fathers strongly encouraged it and others discouraged it.

For example, Origen said that Christians were better than anyone else to govern because their patriotism was not conditional upon personal ambition. Jerome said that God gave two great gifts: The priesthood and the "imperial dignity (government office).

However, there were concerns raised by the Church that being in office may make one subject to participation in judicially injurious violence, torture and execution as well as idolatry.

Prior to the reign of Constantine the Great many believed that Christians should not be involved in government because the policies of the empire were pagan and therefore a Christian would be compromising their faith if they supported them.

The mistake in judgment came when they did not discern the division between the office of government and the pagans who sit in the seat of its power. However, there were many Christians who held public office, maintained spiritual integrity, and performed their civic duties with honesty.

We can view this in two segments. The first was the relation between Church and Empire which was at best tolerant of Christians during the first three hundred years of Church history and the second was from the reign of Constantine through the seventh century.

Antipathy towards the State

In the early days of the Church's growth there was an antipathy towards the state for several reasons:

1. It was viewed as non Christian
2. The Jews who primarily made up the early Christian Church had a hatred of Roman government.
3. The term "free in Christ" was misunderstood by Christians which lead to social and economic discontent.
4. Government crucified Jesus.

The Church view was that the Roman empire would ultimately fall because the Emperors were all pagan idolaters. What they did not foresee was the possibility that God would convert the Emperor as He did with Constantine.

This philosophy discouraged many Christians from entering into public service. We can actually see this same mind set in America. Some people say that politics is dirty. Unfortunately they do not stop to realize that it is not government service that is "dirty" but rather it is the words and actions of those who are in office which subscribe to improper or unethical policies which give it the appearance of being "dirty."

Many of the Church Fathers believed that the state office was given by God, but yet those who held office may have been the evil doers, pagans, etc.

We can see this in the prayer offered by Clemens of Rome who wrote the following prayer asking for God's blessing upon the rulers who were in their positions by God's divine providence:

"Thou Master has given them the authority of royalty by means of thy magnificence and inexplicable power, in order that we, knowing the glory and honor that have been given them by thee, may be submissive to them in no other withstanding thy will.

Give them, Lord, health peace concord stability in order that they may administer without offense the government that has been given them by thee.

For thou heavenly Master, King of the Ages, givest to the sons of man glory and honors and authority over those that are upon the earth; do thou Lord direct their counsel according to what is good and well pleasing in thy sight, in order that they administer piously in peace and gentleness the authority given them by thee may find favor with thee."

The Spread of Church Influence

As the Church's influence spread across the empire, it maintained the general Pauline philosophy that the empire was used by God to provide peace and safety. Christians were taught to obey the laws of the state when consistent with the will of God.

The loyalty, honesty and morality exhibited in the life of believers led many government officials to put Christians in offices of authority and ask for their counsel on matters of state business

One such example is Nilus of Sinai who belonged to a wealthy and illustrious family. His noble birth and personal gifts raised him to the rank of Prefect of the capital. However, his spiritual aspirations led him into the desert to live the monastic life with his son Theodul while his wife and daughter lived in one of the Egyptian convents.

What is of great interest and importance for us to note is that his commitment to the ascetic life did not take him out of communication with the people from the "outside." Along with helping people who sought his counsel, the Emperor also wrote to him asking for his prayers and advice. One such request was met by a sharp rebuke for mistreating John Chrysostom who had been an outspoken critic of the Emperor's policies. (Note: As Bishop of the Church, he routinely addressed the social and governmental issues of the day which he considered a part of his obligations and ministry). Philokalia p.127

Another notable example is with St. Symeon the Stylite. This man would be seen today as eccentric at best and many would think of him as downright crazy. In fact he was "crazy" like a fox.

This man would stand atop a sixty foot pillar in Antioch Syria and preach the gospel all day long. He was so intelligent and respected that even the Emperor would seek his counsel on matters of state business as well as ask for his prayers.

In defining the relationship between the Church and State Bishop Meliton of Sardis wrote, *"Only when Christianity is protected and permitted to develop itself freely, does the Empire continue to preserve its' size and splendor."*

Is it possible that the Founding Fathers drew wisdom from this man when the First Amendment was written that Congress shall not *"...prohibit the free exercise* (of Christianity)?"

Tertullian makes a remarkable comparative between human law based on the philosophy of man as compared to those laws based upon the divine mind of Christ.

> *"How great or effective is human law which can be subverted as opposed to Christian laws which has it's consequences here in this world and eternally?"*

He further states that because Christians have the broader panoramic view of life's consequences which surpass the corporeal they make more sincere attempts at leading a blameless life.

He makes the case that Christians would make better government officials because when tempted in secret out of the sight and knowledge of man they know their deeds and words are seen and heard in God's ears and in His sight.

Thus, the Christian would be more likely to execute the duties of their office with integrity. This would procure the blessings of peace and prosperity from God, presenting a positive role model to people from all religious persuasions and making government more effective.

Tertullian's criticisms of government invariably was directed at the abuse of its authority rather than the institution itself.

14

Government Foundation

The Historian Eusebius wrote that cities and states could not be completed without laws and an order of government. Consequently, the longevity of their existence is dependent upon the moral foundation. If it be based upon God's law then the foundation will not waver and the nation will be secure. If not the foundation will erode and ultimately collapse.

The parable of the wise and foolish men provides an excellent illustration for us. The one built his house on sand and the other built it upon the rock. For a time they both looked stable but when their foundations were tested the house on the rock was the only one that remained(Luke 6:47-49).

The first item of prayer St. Paul teaches to offer is for kings and those in authority for the purpose of having a peaceable life. Thus, the security of governmental rulers is a security to all men within the jurisdiction of their authority. Thus, government is the bulwark of safety for the Church and society.

What then is the content of the prayers we should pray? That their decisions and policies align with all that is right, holy and in complete concord with the will of God. For outside the course and scope of divine absolutes there is confusion and decay, poverty and danger.

If we are called to pray that God's will be done through pagan rulers as in the day of St. Paul then surely it is just as appropriate for God's people to pray that Christians enter into public office where they can apply Christian principles of Christ to public policy. Thereby placing the nation within the four walls of the "house of prosperity, peace and protection."

Who then is most able to minister freedom to those who are bound but those who have a passion to set them free? This does not preclude non Christians from government office as the Bible is abundant with rulers who were not Jews but still lived by the law of God.

Chrysostom condones Christian involvement in politics saying, *"For it is possible both to fulfill to man what is required and to give unto God the things that are due to Him"* (Homily on Romans 13).

He goes on to reference Luke 2:14 which records the birth of Jesus and the exclamation by the Angels when they said, *"Glory to God in the highest and on earth, peace and good will towards man."*

He asserts the rhetorical question that asks how can such a proclamation not affect the government of man. How can there be peace in the heart of mankind and confusion in government?

A distinctive parallel is made between the government and church structure. He explains that laws, courts and judges parallel the kingdom of God and a foreshadow of judgment.

The wrath of God revealed now for correction but at that day it will be for vengeance. The judgments imposed upon the law breakers by the courts enforced by government is for the protection of society and for correction of the wrongdoer. Therefore when laws free the wrongdoer to continue doing wrong a cancer of social degeneration sets in until it becomes terminal.

His explanation of Romans 13:4 teaches that the Bible gives the ruler the name "minister" because his purpose is for the good of the people. By punishing evil he helps good and virtue to excel.

We are drawn to the same conclusion. God set up government and Church to serve the needs of people. Who then is most qualified to be trusted with this authority of government than those who have committed themselves to the principles of God?.

With this attitude and intent the possibility of corruption is lessened because that person is more clearly aware of the eternal consequences to corruption and incompetence. Needless to say the qualifications of the individual elected to public office should be well evaluated by the body politic. Simply because someone adheres to Godly principles does not ensure that he or she would be the most effective government official. However, it does provide the necessary foundation.

Roman Society and the Church

In the early days of the Church the Roman society, being pagan was sharply contrasted with the philosophy and tenets of the Church. This sharp contrast led to Christians being excluded from much of pagan society.

The Christians were seen as anti-social, and at times dangerous fanatics. Many of the secular Humanists in society today see Christianity as a threat and fanatical extremist.

This view ended up serving the purposes of Nero when in 64 A.D. he set Rome on fire and blamed the Christians thus diverting blame from himself to a group of people who had no strength of rebuttal or defense against such charges.

It is much the same today only with more of a sophisticated appeal. Those Christians who assert their constitutional rights in politics and public policy as recently as 1994 and 1995 have been vilified as "dangerous" and bigoted. They have been accused of being intolerant. When, in fact, it is the liberal elite which espouse a socialistic humanistic agenda which enslaves humanity.

This same philosophy towards Christians was adopted by the Emperor Trajan who viewed the Church as being a challenge to the state which was to be obeyed in all matters of civil and religious affairs. Later, other emperors like Diocletian pursued this policy of persecution.

One such famous Christian which Diocletian persecuted was St. George. Yes, this is the famous St. George who slew the dragon. His life testimony of service to the Emperor and Christ is an inspiring one to Christians and non Christians.

The following is an account of his testimony for Jesus Christ as he refused to worship the Emperor as decreed:

St. George

This great miracle worker and martyr lived in the latter part of the third century A.D. during Diocletian's rule of the

Roman Empire. He originally came from the area of Cappadocia and was raised by very pious parents.

When Diocletian started his persecutions against the Christians, Saint George declared himself to be a Christian and thus denied the false idols. he suffered many tortures because of his belief, but never considered renouncing it.

The life of Saint George is a prime example of the life that each Christian should follow...

Saint George, the Great Martyr, was raised in the Christian religion. His father, himself, martyred for his faith. After his father's death, George's mother took him to Palestine where she had some farm land. At a young age, he served in the Roman army under the Emperor Diocletian and was commended many times for his excellent service to the Empire. From the rule of Emperor Decian, until 284 A.D., when Diocletian became Emperor the Christian Church went through a period of peace and prosperity. During that time, the Christians obtained important positions in the government, built many churches and schools, and organized the authoritative structure of the Church. Diocletian gave many of his loyal officers political positions so that he could have the military strength of the Empire on his side.

After Diocletian had suppressed the barbarian tribes which were attacking the Empire and after he had secured its' borders, he began to concentrate on the Empire's internal affairs. Diocletian believed that a state religion could keep an Empire united. Since paganism was the state religion, Diocletian focused his efforts towards the suppression of Christianity.

During the year 303 A.D. Diocletian summoned his aides to meet in Caesarea, a city of the Eastern Roman Empire. He held three general meetings with his aides, instructing them to persecute the Christians. Saint George had shown his excellence while serving in the army, and was among these aides. Diocletian asked them to pledge their allegiance to this cause by making pagan sacrifices as proof of their loyalty. All of the aides pledged their loyalty, except for the Saint. He stood in front of Diocletian and admitted his belief in Christianity, telling the monarch of the Christian teachings and the Godliness of the Crucified Nazarene. The Emperor ordered this Christian taken to prison and that a boulder be placed on his chest as a form of torture. The next morning Diocletian ordered that the prisoner be brought before him for questioning. George stood steadfast and told Diocletian of his belief in the riches of the Kingdom of Heaven.

The Emperor then summoned the executioners to take the Saint and have him bound to the rim of a wheel set with spikes hoping he would sacrifice to the gods to save himself. He refused Diocletian's request and welcomed the chance to martyr for Christ, as his father had done. After praying to God, he heard a voice from heaven say, *"Do not fear, George, I am with you."*

With the help of Christ, the spiked wheel had no effect upon Saint George. When the Saint appeared before Diocletian not only was he unharmed, but an angelic aura had settled about him. Suddenly, two officers of the Roman army, Anatolios and Protoleon, appeared before Diocletian with two thousand soldiers. They admitted their belief in Christ and Diocletian had them all executed.

He then ordered his soldiers to dig a pit and fill it with lime. The Saint was then drenched with water and thrown into the pit. The water and lime would slowly destroy the Saint's body. After three days, Diocletian instructed the soldiers to clear the pit. To the surprise of the soldiers and the Emperor, Saint George sat at the bottom of the pit unharmed. Diocletian demanded to know what type of magic George had used to escape his fate. George answered that he had not used any magic, but that he had been saved by the power of God.

The Emperor then ordered that iron sandals be tied to the feet of the Saint and that he be made to run. As he ran, he was beaten. One of Diocletians advisors, Magnentios, ordered George to perform a miracle. They happened to pass by a tomb of a man who had been dead for many years. Magnentios ordered George to resurrect this man to show the power of his God. After praying for a long time, he rolled the rock away from the tomb and resurrected the dead man.

The by-standers praised the strength of Christ. Diolcetian asked the resurrected man who he was and when he had died. He told Diocletian that he had lived before Christ had come to the Earth and because he was an idolater, he had burned in the fires of hell during all these years. Many idolaters were converted to Christianity because of this great miracle.

Among the people who glorified God and Saint George at the tomb was a farmer named Glecerios. Previously Saint George had resurrected this farmer's oxen, his livelihood. Because the farmer was so outspoken the soldiers murdered him and thus he received the crown of martyrdom.

The next day, Diocletian met with his noblemen to determine St. George's fate. They decided to beat the Saint mercilessly. The Saint nevertheless remained unharmed and retained his angelic appearance. Diocletian was convinced that all of George's miracles were done by magic. He therefore, called upon Athanasius (not the church father Athanasius of Egypt) the magician to break this magic.

Athanasius held two vials in his hands. If the Saint drank the first one, he would go insane, if he drank the second one he would die. The Saint took the first vial and prayed. He drank its' contents and there was no effect. Diocletian still believed that George was a magician; however, Athanasius realized the strength of God and confessed his belief in the Christian God. Athanasius was immediately executed by Diocletian's order.

After seeing the miracles of St. George, Diocletian's wife, the Empress Alexandra, also confessed her belief in Christ. Diocletian imprisoned her. Saint George was returned to prison and dreamed that Christ told him that he would receive the crown of martyrdom and life eternal.

Once again George appeared before Diocletian who ordered that St. George accompany him to the temple and sacrifice to the gods. When they arrived at the temple, St. George made the sign of the cross and the idols were again destroyed. The people and the priests were furious and demanded that Diocletian have the saint executed. Saint George was taken out of the city and as he turned his head toward the executioner, he was beheaded.

George was a man who perfectly mixed Church and State and was effective and proficient to both callings. He brought the light of Christ into a darkened world all the while maintaining perfect loyalty, obedience and service to his emperor.

Shortly after ordering the systematic persecution of Christians Diocletian died a horrible death which was disfiguring and painful. He ended up believing that his edict of persecuting the Christians caused his death.

Could it be possible that while on his death bed he began to ponder the miracles which were done through the life of St. George the Emperor's loyal and valued captain? It may well be that God, in His mercy, allowed Diocletian to reflect upon this to draw him to repentance.

15

Faith in Conflict

Christianity and Roman society came into conflict for several reasons. First, Christianity was exclusive in that it did not accept the pagan deities nor the worship of Caesar as divine. This is important to note because the acceptance of the multiplicity of deities and the worship of Caesar was to unify the empire. This set the Christians in conflict with the empire because of their belief in only one God and there was only one way—Jesus Christ.

Secondly, since Romans believed that their gods protected them they viewed Christianity as the cause of their ills. The Emperor Nero first applied this strategy when he burned Rome and blamed Christians.

As the world comes closer to a one-world government, I am of the belief that attacks on Christianity will increase. Why? For the same reasons it was attacked in early Church history. Namely because Christianity came in direct conflict with that which unified the empire, i.e. worship of the Emperor as divine and it was exclusive of all other religions as being viable.

Here again we see an eerie resemblance between the pagans of the Roman empire and those who are attacking the Church today in twentieth century America. Never have we seen elected officials in the United State so viciously criticize the Christians as when they began to apply their faith and constitutional rights in the public forum.

These attacks have manifested in various ways. An article in the Washington Post ridiculed conservative Christians as "poor, uneducated and easily lead". Other attacks have come through attempts to rescind the tax exempt status of the Roman Catholic church and other evangelical churches because of their stand on abortion and their exercise of constitutional rights. Some attacks have even become violent. Consequently, Christianity will be seen as a divisive religion and therefore a threat to world security, peace and prosperity and unity.

The Book of Revelation speaks of this when it talks of the Antichrist, the false prophet, the beast and the mark of the beast. Anyone who doesn't take the mark will suffer. The Anti-Christ will require all to worship him the same as Caesar did in the days when the Roman Empire ruled the world.

Social World View of Christians

Interestingly the Christian world view was that the individual was to aspire to the highest degree of moral excellence. Furthermore, this world view encouraged Christians to give great consideration to the needs of society as well as the individual.

This social world view lends itself to a tacit endorsement of Christian involvement in politics. For what greater interest in society can be shown except by being its servant in the affairs of state.

For example, President Clinton recently vetoed a bill that would ban the gruesome and inhumane abortion procedure called the Partial Birth Abortion. This diobolical procedure actually thrusts a metal shaft through the back of a child's head and sucks out the brains of the child leading to its' death. If we had a pro-life President this bill would have been signed.

What would have happened if our government leaders believed in personal responsibility and accountability? Possibly we would not have a welfare state that has wasted trillions of taxpayer dollars and "enslaved" so many people in the welfare "prison."

As we look to the leaders of the Christian Church during the first few centuries of its existence we see that a large number of the monastics were men of great intelligence and wealth. Some were government administrators prior to them choosing the monastic life.

At the same time many Christians entered business and government service and their work bore great testimony of the effectiveness and loyalty of Christians to their government and society in the context of their love of Jesus.

I believe that the cause of this dedication to excellence is their knowledge that how they carry out their responsibilities will have a two fold evaluation. The first is the human one. The second is the divine evaluation. This philosophy can be summed up in St. Paul's letter to the Colossians chapter three verses 22-25:

> *"Servants, obey in all things your masters*
> *according to the flesh; not with eye service,*
> *as men pleasers; but in singleness of heart,*

> *fearing God: And whatsoever ye do, do it*
> *heartily, as to the Lord, and not unto men;*
> *Knowing that of the Lord ye shall receive*
> *the reward of the inheritance; for ye serve*
> *the Lord Christ. But he that doeth wrong*
> *shall receive for the wrong which he hath*
> *done; and there is no respect of persons."*

It was and is the view that social well being comes only from God. It is also noteworthy to acknowledge that the Christian social order is directly dependent upon the civic order in twentieth century America.

As we will see in the lives of such saints as Ambrose of Milan, the Christian minister is to herald righteousness to the community and to members of the church. Church history consistently ministers the call to righteousness in the social order and in public office.

Ambrose

Ambrose of Milan who lived in the fourth century A.D. was famous as a politician and preacher. He effectively combined the service to Church and State. He was the first Church leader to use his office successfully to influence civil leaders.

One notable accomplishment of his was when he stood against the reintroduction of the pagan goddess Victory into the Roman Senate House.

Another example of Ambrose impact on society then and now is when he introduced hymn singing in the Church which began when he led a sit-in demonstration against the Empress Justina.

While Christianity is outside the halls of government then government cannot be affected by it.

Early Church View of Politics in General

Even though Christians were obliged to pray for their rulers they were also obliged to exert their influence in the public arena when current government and social standards conflict with theirs.

As I mentioned earlier, in the Roman Empire it was required to worship Caesar as divine by offering incense to him. It was made very convenient for the Christians to make the offering and yet maintain their faith by letting them make the offering in private.

However, to the Christian such an act of sacrilege would be known to God who knows all things and the consequences would be self excommunication from the Church.

An inspiring example of resisting a political requirement which had spiritual consequences was that of Bishop Polycarp. He was implored by government officials to make the sacrifice.

Far from asking him to renounce his faith they tried to convince him that his offering would be in secret. They also said that if he stayed alive he could do so much more work for the gospel and his people.

Bishop Polycarp nevertheless maintained his focus on obedience to Christ and did not take into consideration the deception and influence of the pleasure of this temporal life and the twisted view of his ministry potential presented through the lips of those who did not love Jesus.

He responded by declaring the foundational truth that for decades he had faithfully served the Lord and was never done wrong by him and that he could not renounce Him. He was later sentenced to be burned at the stake and when the fire raged it did not hurt him. He was finally killed by a soldier's spear.

Persecution of Christians in the twentieth century is sure to continue. We may not see the statues of the pagan gods and goddesses but the evil spirits they represented are still working in America today, the spiritual battle is ongoing.

As men and women of faith and moral integrity assert their civil rights, fulfilling their civic responsibilities persecution will be sure to continue to intensify.

I am reminded of something my cousin Brad Nassif said to me one time as we were discussing spiritual warfare. He said, "the devil never fights against the dead."

Opposing Views

Christians who set about fulfilling the Great Commission will run into conflict with the philosophies of humanism. World history has shown and contemporary America testifies that one of two philosophies will govern the society and government of the nation. Either the statutes of secular humanism (the worship of man) or those of the living God will prevail. The two philosophies are mutually exclusive.

As Jesus said, we cannot serve two masters. Neither can a nation. Either man will be the center of all things or it will be God.

As King Solomon says in the Book of Ecclesiastes, there is nothing new under the sun. So it is with "emperor worship" which is tantamount to acknowledging man as the final authority and center of all things.

During the days of the Roman Empire the worship of the Emperor was primarily for the unity of the empire. This same type of "emperor worship" is manifested in acknowledging of man as the final authority in faith morals and conduct.

Any threat to the state religion was a threat to national security because it was believed by the people that the deities kept the empire safe from invaders. To deny them worship would anger them.

Today's threat to the national "deities" of sexual freedom (the goddess Diana) abortion (the god Molech), Bacchus, the god of wine or sensual indulgence, etc. comes from Christians who will not bow the knee to these gods and graven images.

"It is an abomination to kings to commit wickedness: for the throne is established by righteousness" Proverbs 16:12.

"Mercy and truth preserve the king: and his throne is upholden by mercy" Proverbs 20:28.

It is interesting to note that the Roman empire did not consider other religions i.e. Jews and Christians a threat until a Roman citizen became converted. Then they were looked at as a denationalizing influence which then put into question their loyalty to the state. In other words, so long as they did not influence public policy or the status quo they were tolerated. Sound familiar?

Until Christians began to galvanize and assert their political strength they were left alone. Now in the recent past we have seen vicious attacks upon the Christian body politick and Christian leaders for simply exercising their constitutional rights and privileges.

For example, one edition of a national magazine portrayed Ralph Reed (Executive Director of the Christian Coalition) in an imposing, sinister and threatening way. Christian candidates for office have been labeled "stealth candidates" inferring a deceptive agenda. Isn't it interesting that until a few short years ago we rarely if ever witnessed such inflammatory and bigoted slanders upon decent people who simply want a place and opportunity in the public forum?

Even Tertullian, who discouraged government participation by the believer, said that Romans had been deceived by demons which kept them from worshipping the true and living God who, if worshipped would cure the ills of the nation.

In a more dramatic manner St. Ignatius Bishop of Antioch, who was brought before the seat of the Emperor Trajan for the crime of being a Christian directly spoke the truth not concerned about being diplomatic.

Responding to Ignatius' testimony, the Emperor Trajan, in a diplomatic, manner claimed to worship the gods believing that this would be acceptable to Ignatius convincing him to compromise his faith. Ignatius responded by speaking to him the truth in no uncertain terms. He said: Trajan worshipped devils. Trajan then became angry and then in frustration asked, *"Do you carry this Christ with you?"*

Ignatius responded, *"I bear in my body the crucified Christ."*

Thereupon he was sent to the Colosseum to be eaten by lions. His faith was so great that in one of his pastoral letters he requested that no one interfere with what he termed the "completion of his discipleship."

Reign of Decius

Christians also believed that the state could only be preserved by heaven, the difference being that they worshipped God who could deliver and Rome worshipped idols which could not.

During the reign of Decius, Christians did not have enough political influence to convince him that their claims were justified. Ultimately He became a torturous persecutor of Christians who if they would not recant their faith in Jesus they would be persecuted via torture. He sought to crush and obliterate Christians.

When Valerian Succeeded Decius

Valerian became a worse persecutor of Christians than Decius. He banned Christian meetings. Exiled and banished the clergy, and in some cases actually executed them. Aristocratic Christians lost possessions and rank.

During his reign of terror the empire underwent the onslaught of earthquakes, famine, draught, tornadoes, tidal waves and pestilence in which nearly half of the population died. (This sounds like America 1991-1996).

I recall a lady telling me that the posh Hollywood restaurant that she worked at lost nearly 30% of their clientele because they died from A.I.D.S.

This also brings to mind the natural disasters which have occurred in just the last few years bringing a unique parallel to what occurred under Valerian's reign and what is happening to America as she had turned away from the moorings of the law of the Lord.

We have seen raging fires consume southern California followed by torrential rains. America's resources are being deleted by the burgeoning national debt and hurricanes which have come in record numbers. In May of 1996 we are hearing about the devastating effects of tornadoes in the midwest, hail the size of grapefruit falling from the sky in Texas, and an earthquake in Seattle, Washington. Could God's creation be sending us a message?

Constantine The Great

In recounting the story of Constantine we see how God moved in a sovereign manner on this man who was a pagan. Constantine, heard that enemies he was about to battle were using the magic arts to prepare for the battle. He then called upon the "Supreme God" to help him. As he recounts to the historian Eusebius, he then saw in the noon day sun the sign of the cross with the words: "By This Sign Conquer."

While sleeping that night Constantine had a dream. In that dream Jesus told him to affix the sign of a cross to the soldiers' breastplates and shields.

In 312 A.D. the battle for at the Milvian Bridge was fought and won by Constantine. Thus we see the manifestation of overt divine intervention in the affairs of state. (Talk about Christian involvement in politics!) Later Constantine issued the Edict of Milan which gave permanent freedom of religion to the Christians.

After his victory at the Battle of the Milvian Bridge Constantine made a conscious decision to pursue the manifestation of "true religion" in the life of the Church through the offices of the state. *"...what higher duty have I as than to destroy error and ...so cause all to offer to all mighty God through religion honest concord and due worship?"*

Some have criticized Constantine's role in the relation between the Church and state. However, I believe that if we were living in those days we would welcome the conversion of the pagan empire to Christ and the Edict of Milan in 313 A.D. which secured religious freedom for Christians.

Through King Constantine the Church was offered protection throughout the empire which greatly helped in the spread of the gospel. Likewise, the morality of the Church was communicated to the offices of government. Even though there were concerns from time to time the Church and state benefited each other.

I find it interesting that God converted the Roman empire instead of destroy it. The move of God came through the offices of human government and not apart from it. This seems to follow a pattern.

For nearly five hundred years after the birth of Jesus Christians were often accused by pagans of being the source of the national problems because they would not worship the deities.

Specifically, the fall of the Western Empire was attributed to the Christians refusal of worshipping the deities.

To this philosophy St. Augustine said that in fact it was the Roman gods which brought this disaster upon the empire because the worship of them did nothing to prevent the Roman Republic from being destroyed by immorality. Rome had no precepts of morals and rule of life.

St. Augustine said, *"It is apparent that when the Republic was being destroyed by profligate manners, its gods did nothing to hinder its destruction by the direction or correction of its' manners, but rather accelerated its destruction by increasing the demoralization and corruption that already existed."*

We can also see this in Ezekiel where God said that He would make their land a barren wasteland for all the wicked deeds the Israelites had done. Ezekiel 6:14.

St. Augustine continues to say in "The City of God" that those who complain against Christians, and use them as a scape goat for the destructive effects of their immorality, do in fact want to live in luxury and without restraint. They desire a state of Hedonism, Epicurean and lust. This sounds like liberalism in 1996 America.

Christianity Protected The People

Augustine further states that when the Barbarians invaded the country the people who took refuge in Christian temples actually were protected. The grace and favor of God was upon the Christians. Otherwise why weren't the Christians temples destroyed like the others?

16

Morality—Moral Absolutes: The Pillars of Government and Society

When a nation has divested itself of moral absolutes, it then becomes vulnerable to every theory, philosophy, and moral depravity that previously was resisted by the fortress of truth.

When Israel forsook her relationship with God He sent Prophets to warn of the impending consequences. Through these prophets God kept calling them to repentance. However, Israel was under the delusion of a false sense of security because there was no impending danger.

The Prophet Jeremiah wrote of this experience when he was called by God to speak forth the word of the Lord to Israel when she had sought after *"the imagination of their own evil heart"* (Jeremiah 11:8;16:2). When a call for repentance was ignored, then the judgment day was set.

Everything seemed fine until they rebelled against God. They would not hear His call to repentance. His judgment fell and they were taken into captivity.

The consequences of rebellion against God may take several years to manifest. We can see evidence of this in the account of when Christ cursed the fig tree. (Mark 11:13; 14:2). It wasn't until the next morning after He cursed it that the apostles saw that it had dried up from its' roots.

The reason why God doesn't immediately send retribution upon disobedient people is because He wants them to turn from their sin to live and not die. The same as a parent warns their child not to take rides from strangers.

As one of the Church Fathers, St. Maximus the Confessor said, *"He who loves God leads the life of an angel on earth...He who fears the Lord has humility as his constant companion and, by its reminding, ascends to love and gratitude to God."*

Esther's Eyesight Hindered

The Book of Esther records the life of a young Jewish girl who God favored in the eyes of the king and she was made queen. The kings Prime Minister hated the Jews and schemed to destroy them. Mordecai (Esther's uncle) and the Jews put on sackcloth and ashes and he sat at the gate of the king.

Because it was not lawful for anyone to sit in the king's gate in sackcloth and ashes Esther brought to Mordecai new clothes. In this she responded to the immediate concern without understanding the long ranging one which had greater consequences for the Jews, herself and the king.

Instead of going to Mordecai to discover the reason for the sackcloth and ashes, she immediately tried to deal with the problem when she said to him: "Do not incur the wrath of the king." When in fact the greater wrath of the king had been decreed.

Fortunately for the Jews and for the future generations who read the Book of Esther, she listened to Mordecai. Esther then understood why he was in sackcloth and ashes, and actively responded to his request for her intercession with the king. Had she not listened to him, the Book of Esther would not be written as we know it and we would be deprived of the testimony of her life.

This reminds me of the deceptive nature of wealth, power and easy living which can affect the individual person as well as a nation in general. Left unguarded it can cloud the spiritual perception of truth. Illusion and delusion inverts the judgment of right and wrong ultimately leading to the occasional practice of sin. This can lead to the continuing practice of sin the end result of which numbs a person's conscience to a point where they feel no guilt. Finally, this leads to God's ultimate judgment.

Mark the Ascetic lived in the fourth and fifth century. He was known for his great humility and keen sensitivity to spiritual warfare. He said about sin:

> *"The devil presents small sins to us as
> insignificant in our eyes, for otherwise
> he cannot lead us to great sins."*

A prime example of this on a national basis is in regard to abortion. In 1973 abortion on demand legalized baby killing. Once this was accepted then gruesome methods such as the partial birth abortion came to be used. This technique brings the child out of the womb except for the head which then had a shaft inserted into it and sucks the brain out, killing the baby.

What is equally distressing and concerning to me is that this year in 1996 the United States Congress passed legislation banning the partial birth abortion however, President vetoed the bill.

What lurks in the heart of a man who has the opportunity to save babies from this tortuous and insidious death and refuses to do so? I can't imagine.

The Ways We Sin or Serve God

There are three methods in which we sin or serve God. Those ways are by word deed and thought. The thought, once dwelt upon, becomes the desire of the heart. The word is the heart's intent and the deed is the word made manifest in action.

Word

King Solomon, said that *"Life and death are in the power of the tongue and they that love it shall eat the fruit thereof"* Proverbs 18:2.

Jesus says that our spoken words not only have a potent effect in the spiritual and natural kingdoms but they have an eternal impact on the state of our soul.

> *"But I say unto you, that every idle word*
> *that men shall speak, they shall give account*
> *thereof in the day of judgment. For by thy*
> *words thou shalt be justified, and by thy*
> *words thou shalt be condemned"* Matthew 12:37.

In my early years walking with the Lord I was visiting Mt. Paran Chuch of God, an honorable and spiritual ministry. The day I was visiting they were having a fund raising project and asking for pledges. During the whole service I had been deeply touched by the presence of the Lord.

I felt that the Lord was leading me to commit $300.00 per month for four years. After one year of making the monthly payments, I had a change of mind and felt that the commitment that I made was on a carnal level and then stopped the payments.

Two years later I sold my business. Then the Lord actually spoke to me and said... *"Remember the vow?"* I said ... "But that was in the 'flesh.'"

The Lord responded: *"But you made a vow. I expect you to keep it."*

I did keep it too. I had to write a check for $10,800.00, but at least I kept my word just like Jesus does when He makes a promise.

Spoken words of position that either align or conflict with the will of God will produce the fruits of God's blessing or His judgment. In either case we are the ones who bring either the judgment or blessing to pass.

A dramatic example of this is the story of David in I Chronicles chapter 20 and 21. The first word recorded was that Satan rose up against Israel. How? He planted the thought in David's mind to number the tribes of Israel contrary to God's word.

General Joab saw that David was beginning to trust the strength of his armies instead of the Lord. He spoke up to

David but was overruled. Consequently Satan attacked David's thought process leading him to sin by his word and the action of his authority. This resulted in the deaths of 70,000 Israelites.

We Can't Be Silent: It's Too Loud

In Numbers, chapter 30, the Lord says that if a woman makes a vow and her husband does not know about it and then later hears of it, he can annul the vow. However, if, upon hearing the vow he says nothing to the contrary, that vow will stand. Therefore knowledge of the vow without an express annulment of it is a validation of the vow. Therefore words spoken and unspoken have the same weight of accountability as the other.

Deed

The Book of Psalms says:
> *"Who shall ascend into the hill or who shall*
> *stand in his holy place? He that hath clean hands and a*
> *pure heart; who hath not*
> *lifted up his soul unto vanity nor*
> *sworn deceitfully"* Psalms 24:3,4.

Here we see the "word," "thought," and "deed" addressed. Each has the effect of leading the person into communion with God or keeping him out. Jesus taught this principle through the parable of the two sons in Matthew 21-28-31.

The two men were given the same instructions. One said he would be obedient but did nothing and the other said he would not be obedient and yet was. Jesus illustrates that the true test of whether a person is doing the will of the Father is by what he does or does not do.

Many of us give more weight to our words as opposed to our actions in defining our faith. The words of the Apostle James are not taken seriously when he says: *"Faith if it have not works is dead"* James 2:17.

Out of all the evangelical Christians that voted in the 1992 presidential campaign twenty eight per cent voted for Bill Clinton! They did this despite the depravity of the positions of the Clinton ticket on such issues as abortion and homosexuality.

Even though most would say they oppose abortion and homosexuality they, in fact, have spoken approval by the mere fact that they knew Clinton's position and yet endorsed him.

Such an act is of great spiritual severity. It is so severe that those who voted for Clinton will have to give account for every abortion performed under his administration, as well as the detrimental effects of homosexuality which has been endorsed by the administration.

One may ask what the believer should do if all the candidates held the same positions on the fundamental moral issues. What is the next course of action in deciding who to support? Should the believer just not vote?

I was faced with this decision in the last election for the office of Mayor of Los Angeles. Both candidates endorsed the pro abortion position, albeit one was more restrictive than the other. It was a real dilemma for me. After seeking the mind of the Lord it occurred to me that I needed to vote for the person who was most closely aligned with the pro life position.

To what extent does the believer apply this principle of vote responsibility? When there are no perfect candidates. Who should be supported? (If any?)

This can be seen in Paul's letter to the Romans where Paul expounds on this principle in reference to the day of rest and the eating of meat. In both instances the believer is left to his own choice with the caution not to allow their freedom to be a stumbling block to others.

In the world of government and politics there are political issues which we are permitted the leeway of decision without violating biblical standards of faith and conduct. Some are the ratification of treaties, transportation policies, etc.

However, when a particular policy professed by a candidate is clearly anti- biblical or blasphemous then we are directed not to endorse such a messenger. An example of this is in the case of abortion and immorality (e.g. homosexuality).

Thought

The third method that affects the person and ultimately a nation is through thoughts which can lead to rebellion or obedience to God.

In Ezekiel 28:6,7 God spoke to the King of Tyre rebuking him for his arrogance and pride. Interestingly, he also spoke to him in terms that would only refer to the devil. Referring to Satan's appearance before his fall i.e. *"anointed cherub with the tabrets and beauty."*

Why would God say such a thing when speaking to a human being? This brings us to conclude that Satan had so greatly influenced the king that when the Lord spoke to one He was speaking to the other. Here we see the interaction of the spiritual and natural worlds.

> *"Because...thou hast said, I am a God, I sit*
> *in the seat of God ...yet thou art a man, and*
> *not God, thou set thine heart as the heart*
> *of God: Therefore thus saith the Lord God; because*
> *thou hast set thine heart as the heart of God;*
> *Behold, therefore I will bring strangers upon*
> *thee...and they shall draw their swords against*
> *the beauty of thy wisdom...Thou has been in*
> *Eden the garden of God; every precious stone was*
> *thy covering...Thou art the anointed Cherub...thou*
> *wast perfect in thy way ...till iniquity was found*
> *in thee"* Ezekiel 28:1-19.

Thus, we can see that through word deed and thought, commission of sin is as serious for one who sees it being done and says nothing as well as the one who practices it.

Politically Active: To Be or Not to Be

We know that political activity is a method to speak out on the issues affecting the local community, nation and the world. Silence and inactivity is acceptance of the status quo.

Our political system has the ability to change the actions of a nation and third by electing men and women of upright character reflecting sound judgment, honesty and candor.

One might say that righteousness can apply to moral issues but how can this thought process apply to such political issues as taxes, appropriations for different programs, foreign policy, etc.

First sound judgment in what we call non moral issues can definitely result from the mental, emotional and spiritual disposition of those who are possessed of a high moral integrity and principles. Remember, the mind of God also reflects good business judgment as well as sound moral values.

We need to keep in mind that man is subject to mistakes and errors made as a result of sincere efforts to do what is right. For example, several years ago there was a man who was in a business relationship that was nonproductive to say the least. The counsel that the Lord gave him was that if he would continue to serve Jesus and walk in righteousness He would take the rubble of the past and pave the highway for the future.

Joseph, Honor and Integrity

A case in point is in the story of Joseph as well as other godly men who were astute in business. These men were given authority over the king's business because of their high degree of intelligence and sound judgment rooted in their deep moral commitment to truth and righteousness. Genesis 41:33-44; Daniel 2:46-48; Proverbs 22:29.

Because Joseph walked in the righteousness of God he was endowed by the Lord with favor (Genesis 39:2). While he was in prison after being falsely accused of immoral behavior by Potiphar's wife, Joseph interpreted the dreams of two of Pharoah's servants. One was a baker whose dream foretold of his death. The butler's dream foretold of him being reinstated to his position as Pharaoh's butler.

When Pharaoh had his dreams about the seven fat and lean cows and the seven fat and lean ears of corn and he could not interpret the dream he became distraught. Finally, his butler told him about Joseph and the dream interpretation.

Pharaoh called for Joseph to interpret the dreams. Pharoah believed him and Egypt prepared for the famine. The effects of the famine were "worldwide." People from all nations were saved from starvation and death by being able to buy food from Egypt. (Genesis 41:54-end; 42:1)

It is critical to note that it was the butler who brought the Pharaoh and Joseph together which resulted in the salvation of the whole world. He did not have to get involved in the political issues of Pharaoh's dreams (everything that involved Pharaoh was political) but he did. To have given Pharaoh advice which could prove inaccurate, especially in such a dramatic issue, could result in death. Remember, the butler was not a Hebrew or a man who knew God. He put his life on the line and he did not even know for what except hoping to see Pharaoh's dreams interpreted.

He could have said to himself, yes Joseph was right about my dream but what if he is wrong about Pharaoh's dreams? I could be executed for bringing him to Joseph. Thank God, that the butler got involved in government affairs and recommended that Pharoah speak to Joseph.

When Joseph was summoned to Pharaoh he did not say that he felt God's people shouldn't be involved in politics. Rather, he responded and God gave him the dream interpretation. It is wise to keep in mind that Pharaoh had the power of life and death in his word. If Pharaoh did not like Joseph's interpretation he could have had him and the butler executed.

However, Joseph had built a strong relationship with God and knew that the interpretation was accurate.

It was God's spiritual gift that caused Joseph to be promoted to Prime Minister of the Egyptian empire. This opened the door for the wisdom of God to be poured out upon the entire empire and world bringing forth a blessing to all peoples and saved the world from starvation.

Joseph was made Prime Minister and through the Lord working in him all of Egypt, the Jews and the world was blessed. What would have happened if Joseph felt he shouldn't have gotten involved?

In conclusion; the move of God through Joseph would not have occurred unless the butler allowed himself to be the connecting factor which joined the man of God who possessed the wisdom of God with the government of Egypt through Pharaoh.

Finally, we need to act like the butler and assert ourselves in the political arena to promote the *"Josephs"* of today to government office.

Who knows whether we would be used by God to bring peace, health and freedom to ourselves and the world just as God did through Joseph as he was promoted to Pharaoh by the butler.

Who knows if God has called some of us to be the "Joseph's" and "Butlers" of America. When pondering whether to be involved in politics just keep in mind...the butler did it.

17

Moral Breakdown

When a nation (or person) forsakes the morals of the Judeo-Christian ethic that nation will soon experience the degeneration of its' culture in all aspects from academic to economic. The first step to this degeneration is when they reject God as the benefactor of their rights, strength and prosperity.

An example of the process of decay can be seen when a plant having been carefully nurtured, given sunshine, good soil and watered, suddenly is deprived of all these necessary ingredients of life. The danger can not be seen initially, one would not see a noticeable change in the appearance of the plant. However, through the continued deprivation of those things which give it life the plant begins to decay. First the root, then the stalk and finally the whole plant.

We can see this more evident with regard to the fall of man in the Garden. The Bible records that Eve saw that the forbidden tree was appealing to the eye, good to eat and something to make one wise. Thus, her first mistake was putting herself in a position to dwell upon that which could bring her harm.

This resulted in Adam joining the act of rebellion. This one act of defiance led to the death of all mankind and creation as well as to themselves.

God told Adam that the day in which he would eat of the Tree of the Knowledge of Good and Evil he would surely die. However, the Bible says that Adam lived to be over nine hundred years old. On the surface there seems to be a contradiction. Not so.

Athanasius of Egypt, is one of the great Church Fathers. He spearheaded the defense of the doctrine of the deity of Christ at the First Ecumenical Council of Nicea in 325 A.D. In that regard he wrote the book, *"On The Incarnation Of The Word."* In this book Athanasius writes that when Adam committed the sin of eating the forbidden fruit he did die that day just as the Lord said.

However, Adam's death started in the spiritual realm when he was expelled from the Garden of Eden. He was denied access to the Tree of Life and intimate fellowship with the Fountainhead of Life, the Lord Himself. Secondly, His mental thought process went from being perfect (Adam was able to use 100% of his brain power e.g. when he named all the animals of the earth...and remembered them) to degenerative. Finally, cessation of life itself, the spirit being separated from the body. The body being buried then decays into extinction.

As with the plant, as with Adam and Eve, as with mankind so it is with any nation that turns itself from the Fountainhead of Life, Jesus Christ and the precepts which He gives us.

A second event which occurs when a nations moral values decay is that the work ethic begins to suffer. The work attitude inverts itself from the philosophy of serving the employer and the customer to wanting more pay for less productivity. As well, it can be translated into simply not being the most productive.

Third, the welfare state begins to grow. The non-productive begin to outnumber the producers. The human spirit begins to be enslaved to lethargy and laziness.

On the other hand the Christian philosophy focuses on the salvation, regeneration and productivity of the individual. The dual purpose of seeing the individual use their gifts and talents to the maximum for personal fulfillment while at the same time making a positive contribution to society.

> *"Charge them that are rich in this world,*
> *that they be not high minded, nor trust in*
> *uncertain riches, but in the living God,*
> *who giveth us richly all things to enjoy*
> *That they do good, that they be rich in good*
> *works, ready to distribute, willing to*
> *communicate"* I Timothy 6:17,18.

As I think on this I am reminded of my father who, at twelve years old, came to the United States from a small village in Lebanon. He grew up in Cedar Rapids, Iowa. After the eighth grade he quit school to help support his family. With his eighth grade education he sold newspapers for a nickel. Barely able to speak English he worked hard, had faith in God and was kind and generous to the less fortunate.

Through living the virtues of a high moral standard and hard work he became a successful businessman, real estate developer and philanthropist. His community service to the city of Cedar Rapids, Iowa and throughout the country brought him commendations and acknowledgments from all sectors of society.

In 1956 he went back to his village in Lebanon to help his family and people in various ways. His efforts were recognized by the Lebanese government when they bestowed upon him the Medal of Honor for his philanthropic work. He was the host of many heads of state, including the Prince of Kuwait. He was respected for his success and honored for his compassion.

There are five things I remember most about my father. First, he was committed to his church publicly and privately. Secondly, he was committed to his family. Third he was a hard worker. Fourth, he was involved in the political process. Last but not least, he was always sensitive to those who were less fortunate.

When we were growing up he would tell us that he graduated from the school of the "hard knocks" and that he never wanted us to forget from where he came. Keeping that in mind he wanted us to remember the poor and less fortunate. He also wanted us to get a good education and work hard.

I recall that when I was twelve years old he required me to work every Saturday night washing glasses at our steak house supper club. It was a very famous restaurant. Many celebrities such as John Wayne, Dorothy McGuire, John Glenn and Frank Aletter ate there.

One night I was sitting in the booth next to my father when a friend of his came over to visit him. He made comment to my father that he had me working. My father's response was to say, *"I'm teaching him the value of a dollar."*

Responsibility, hard work and sensitivity to the poor, were the foundations that he taught. From this and his personal involvement in civic and government affairs I later understood the civic responsibility we all have to our nation, city and family.

The lessons of responsibility were received. During my adult years I started a company with a $250.00 loan from my sister and sold it just seven years later. This gave me the time to study the Bible. Later I worked for Mr. Bert Boeckmann, the Owner of several automobile dealerships, one of which is the largest Ford dealership in the world.

Interestingly, my responsibilities were to set up and maintain a purchasing department. This resulted in dramatic savings and increased productivity. Additionally I would evaluate proposals for business investments.

This productivity can be directly attributed to two very important factors in my life. First, the teachings and life of my father who taught me the value of the dollar and reward of hard work. Secondly, my faith and relationship in Jesus Christ who literally guided me in all business affairs as well as my personal life.

The Church is the fountainhead of the precepts which extol the belief in the reward of hard work. However, during the last thirty years there was such an attempt at equality in the work place, that personal excellence and achievement became less important. It was more important what color skin a person had rather than the quality of their product and the cost they were charging.

When my father came to America from Lebanon there was only one thing provided to him . An opportunity. He was not the exception he was the consistent rule. Many members of my family became successful business and government leaders. Their principles stood on the philosophy of fairness, equality and hard work.

18

Faith in Action

What can happen when adherents to the Judeo-Christian ethic act upon their convictions? A great deal. For example, in recent years we have seen a parallel between recent rulings which have distorted the original intent of the Constitution and the nation's diversion from the Judeo Christian ethic. For example, we have seen the United States Supreme Court make decisions which have given First Amendment protection to some forms of pornography.

Now, because God fearing people such as those working with the Enough is Enough Campaign decided to get involved in the governmental process we have seen dramatic results which is succeeding in lifting the protections and eliminating this social cancer.

Another example was to interpret the principle of Separation of Church and State as being a Constitutional doctrine. Thus, compelling the decision to disallow prayer in the schools.

Once again, thanks to a great group of Christians working with the American Center for Law and Justice we have seen successful litigation which is returning the freedom of religion to school children. Additionally, Senators and Congressmen joined together to pass the Equal Access Law designed to eliminate discrimination against Christians in public life.

These two examples testify of the positive influence that Christians can make when they apply their faith and moral principles to government affairs. They combined their prayers with action...and got results.

Thinking of this reminds me of a story I heard where a Christian man was sitting in his house when it began to rain. The rains were so severe that the streets were immersed in water. As the rains continued the flood waters reached the porch of his house.

After praying for the Lord to send help, a man in a small row boat came by and offered to take the man to safety. The man graciously declined his offer and continued praying for the Lord's help.

The rains continued and the flood swelled to the point where the man had to climb to the top of the house to avoid drowning. Then he saw a helicopter flying by. Seeing him, the pilot came down and offered to take him to dry ground. He declined continuing in his stand of faith that God would deliver him from the floods.

The flood waters finally overwhelmed him and he died. Upon entering heaven's gates he saw Jesus and asked Him why He didn't save him in answer to his stand of faith and prayer.

Jesus replied, *"I sent you a row boat and a helicopter. What more did you want?"*

I believe that this is the unfortunate thought process of many Christians and Christian leaders in America today. They keep praying for God to do something about the ills facing the nation such as the family breakdown, drug abuse, teenage pregnancy, governmental corruption etc. but yet they will not take the action necessary to make the changes.

The irony is that if anyone owning a home or property had their taxes go up at an excessive rate surely they would be quick to protest in hopes of reducing the tax. Why would there be such a prompt response? Because people would be faced with the problem on a personal level and in an immediate manner. There would be no opportunity to ignore the consequences of the problems as there would be on issues like abortion, term limits, etc.

Are we prepared to take the same action to elect honorable men and women to positions of government office as we would to reduce our tax assessment? Would we be equally prepared to protest the murder of innocent little children who want to be born as we would to protest the high rates of our income taxes?

Do we have our priorities in order or are we falling into the same trap as the "me" generation did in the sixties and seventies? Are we prepared to re-focus our national and world view to realign with the focus and direction of the Founding Fathers of our nation? Building the foundation instead of tearing it down.

When the relationship between Church and State is balanced and in proper order as the Founding Fathers intended, we see that they can be productive partners. The government protects the rights of the individual to be creative and the

Church provides the conscience and moral foundation for their national expression.

An excellent example of how the Church and secular segments of society can partner together to the mutual benefit of the nation can be seen in regard to the film industry. Until the early 1960's the Protestant and Catholic Churches had offices in Hollywood monitoring the content of the films produced. There was a good relationship between the Church and Hollywood. They worked together to ensure that the films were consistent with sound moral ethics as well as high creative content.

Unfortunately in the early 1960's those church offices were closed creating a moral void in the entertainment industry. Even worse, this came at a time when the drug culture came on the American scene. In the 1970's the "Me" generation joined the drug culture to dominate American politics and society. Sex, violence and drugs became the themes for Hollywood films.

Statesmen vs. Politician

The person who bases their decisions upon the morals of the Judeo-Christian ethic possess the understanding that there will be two types of accounting to be given. The first is the immediate effect of the decisions upon the nation. The second is the eternal effect upon that person.

Noah Webster eloquently states this principle when he said:
> *"The principles of all genuine liberty, and of wise laws and administrations are to be drawn from the Bible and sustained by its' authority. The man therefore who weakens*

> *or destroys the divine authority of that*
> *book may be accessory to all the public*
> *disorders which society is doomed to suffer."*

This same principle was reaffirmed by President Abraham Lincoln. During the Civil War President Lincoln, responding to a question as to whether God was on the Union side, said:

> *"I am not at all concerned about that,*
> *for I know that the Lord is always on*
> *the side of the right. But is my*
> *constant anxiety and prayer that I and*
> *this nation should be on the Lord's side."*

President Lincoln probably was first made aware of this principle by reading the Scripture in Joshua:

> *"And it came to pass when Joshua was by*
> *Jericho, that he lifted up his eyes and*
> *looked and, behold, there stood a man over*
> *against him with his sword drawn in his hand:*
> *and Joshua went unto him, and said unto him,*
> *Art thou for us, or for our adversaries?*
> *And he said, Nay; but as captain (prince)*
> *of the host of the Lord am I now come.*
> *And Joshua fell on his face to the earth,*
> *and did worship, and said unto him, What*
> *saith my lord unto his servant?..."* Joshua 5:14,15.

By these Scriptures we know that God's sole loyalty is to the truth. When mankind aligns themselves to the truth in righteousness then they align themselves with the Lord and all his blessings and protection.

The paramount illustration as to God's commitment to truth is the fact that He was willing and did sacrifice His own son in order to comply with his word and yet provide for the salvation of mankind.

We can get a greater appreciation of this in following the record of God's relationship with the Jews when they came out of Egypt.

God made it very clear that his blessings are conditional upon the children of Israel living in obedience to the word of God and not worshipping other gods. He expects his bride, Israel, to remain faithful to her "husband" who betrothed her in covenant relationship:

> *"Therefore you shall keep the commandments of the Lord thy God, to walk in his ways and to fear him. For the Lord thy God brings thee into a good land...And it shall be, if thou do at all forget the Lord thy God, and walk after other gods, and serve them, I testify against you this day that ye shall surely perish. As the nations which the Lord destroyeth before your face, so shall ye perish; because you would not be obedient..."* Deuteronomy 8:5-20.

Thoughout the Scriptures God demonstrates that He wants us to be obedient in order to enter into the fullness of His mercy and blessings. What may be perceived as threats for disobedience are actually words of warning of the natural consequences of those actions. God is, so to speak, posting warning signs on the highway of life. These signs are the same for individuals as they are for nations.

God is the source of life. To turn away from Him is to turn away from life to death. Adam and Eve experienced this when they were told of the consequences of eating of the tree. To eat of the tree is rebellion and rebellion takes one out of fellowship with God who is light and life.

The writer of Proverbs speaks of this when he, by inspiration of the Holy Spirit, writes:

> *"You rejected my advice and paid no attention when I warned you. Now, you will eat the fruit of what you have done,... sin and self satisfaction bring destruction and death to stupid fools. But if you listen to me you will be safe and secure without fear of disaster"* Proverbs 1:30-33.

The prophet Ezekiel also reflects the heart of God when the Lord tells him to say to the nation of Israel,

> *"...They have lost all hope of survival and they blame me. Tell them that as surely as I am the living Lord God, I don't like to see wicked people die. I enjoy seeing them turn from their sins and live. So if the Israelites want to live, they must stop sinning and turn back to me"* Ezekiel 33:10-11.

As it is with a man or woman so it is for a nation. It is of great importance for people of faith to be active in determining the nation's course. It's a matter of life or death.

The American Tradition In Jeopardy

America has had a tradition of faithfulness to God. Primarily in the last thirty years she has begun to look at herself as the final authority on faith, morals and conduct.

Over thirty million babies have been killed under the distorted view of the fourteenth amendment, prayer in the public schools was banned under the distorted view of the First Amendment.

Because the Church has the knowledge and understanding of the Lord and His will then she will be held accountable to the Lord if America continues on the path of idolatry and self worship subsequently bringing judgment from God.

> *"Son of man, I have made thee a watchman*
> *unto the house of Israel; therefore hear*
> *the word at my mouth, and give them warning*
> *from me..."* Ezekiel 3:17,18.

I believe that Edmund Burke was inspired by God when he made the timeless statement of wisdom in saying, *"All that is necessary for evil to triumph is for good men to do nothing."*

There are those who say that government cannot and should not legislate morality. I submit to you that every law on the books today is an attempt to legislate morality. Our nation has laws against stealing and murder because it is determined that both are immoral in that they impose a denial of the civil rights upon the victim. The moral standards used were the ten commandments.

Several years ago I heard a profound statement on a Christian radio station. The gentleman who spoke said, *"There are over three million laws on the books today...All trying to enforce the Ten Commandments."*

Some legislators justify their reason for being hypocritical on such issues as abortion, being "personally against it" but do not want to "impose their morality upon someone else." I submit that this thought process is the most devious in that the foundation of this type of person is easily moved and has no substance of morality. Even so, their final vote on various legislation is an act (intended or unintended) of determining moral standards of behavior for the implied purpose of protecting and prospering the city, state and nation.

The moral character of government is made up of the moral character of those people who sit in the office of those government institutions. Those people derive their morals from the society in which they live.

There are two opposing forces at work in society throughout all ages of human history. The forces of good and the forces of evil. Each are vying for the minds and hearts of the people. The conscience of America has always been the Church.

When the conscience of America (the Church) became seared with worldliness, comfort and complacency, the immutable principles of the Gospel became distorted, fomenting a breakdown of the family unit. The consequences produced by the "cause and effect" of natural law have begun to set in.

Mankind needs always to live in accordance with natural law as established by the Lord and referred to by the Declaration of Independence. To do otherwise would be like someone desiring to jump off a building having a deep belief that they won't fall because that is their belief. Reality says that no matter how great or sincere one's belief is, the law of gravity will cause them to fall. Thus, the natural consequences of our actions.

Only those who adhere to the truths and principles of God which lead to health, peace and prosperity will apply them to life and the nation. Only those who acknowledge the Lordship of God in the affairs of man will submit the nation's public policies to Him.

Since God reigns in the governments of men, then it is logical that God is pleased for His people to participate in the political process and/or serve in government office.

Keith Fournier, Executive Director for The American Center for Law and Justice, quotes Alexander Solzynitsen as saying that "...*the prime culprit to the decline of America as a great civilization is in its apathy and laziness causing its people to forsake the use of their freedom that is a birthright. What is this birthright? The right to speak out verbally, writing or in the casting of a ballot.*"

Mr. Solzenitsen is well qualified to speak to this issue. He has seen the fruits of a philosophy and political system that seeks to imprison the body, soul and spirit of mankind. He has paid the price. He has earned our respect and our attention to his words of admonition.

19

God: Abortion's Other Victim!

The abortion debate has become one of the most contentious issues of today. The primary focus of the Pro life position is on the fact that abortion is the intentional taking of a human life. On the other hand the Pro abortion advocates base their positions on what is perceived as a woman's constitutional right to "privacy" based upon the 1973 Roe vs. Wade Supreme Court Decision. We see two primary persons directly affected by abortion, the woman having the abortion and the child being aborted.

In reality there is another person who is directly involved in the experience of abortion. That person is God Himself. When God is brought into the debate it is usually from a theological, academic point of view rather from a personal one. This, leaves several questions unanswered.

What does God experience when an abortion ocurrs? What is in His heart concerning the issue itself? What will be the consequences of our actions or inactions?

When an abortionist enters into a mother's womb to perform an abortion they have invaded the "Holy of Holies" of the mother's body. This is where God is nurturing, loving and forming His baby, His *"living sacrifice."* Imputing into the child God's divine plan which no one else will have.

As the abortionist's instruments of death rip the child from God's arms the baby is torn into pieces. The baby's blood is thrown into the face of God Himself.

(NOTE: *Though abortion takes various forms, the results are the same: The blood is spilled and the baby is torn whether by saline solution, forceps etc.*)

Imagine, if you can, a mother and father sitting in their home, the mother nursing their newborn baby and the father looking on in love for his child.

Suddenly, an intruder enters the home, rips the baby from the arms of its' mother. He ties up the parents. The child is then mutilated and killed as they watch in horror. The aftermath is too gruesome to describe. Then he calmly walks out the door.

Can there be any words to describe their pain? Are there any words that can describe their rage? What will they do to avenge the diabolical act of horror?

If a parent would have these feelings if one of their children were so killed, how much greater wrath, rage, anger and vengeance will God pour out upon a people who have inflicted this same fiendish and infernal act upon Himself over thirty million times?

Abortion Is An Act Of Devil Worship

Abortion is an act of devil worship. The abortionist is the "high priest," the nurses attending him are the "deaconesses of sin" and the womb of the mother is transformed from being a fountain of life into the "altar" of death.

When the child is killed, the manifest presence of God leaves the womb. The spirit of death enters and the door to the mother's life and heart becomes open for demons and evil spirits to ravage her emotionally, physically and spiritually.

In pondering upon such a heart-wrenching revelation, I began hearing what may be described as the wailing of the voice of the Lord crying out:

"How long shall I hold back my wrath from a nation that has destroyed my 'inheritance', my babies, my children? How long? For the cup of my anger is about to be poured out upon this nation, for the abominations done.

I have defended my people and this nation from earthly and spiritual enemies. I have bestowed bountiful blessings upon this land. They have become fat with the fruit of the land and now they show their "love" for me by murdering my innocents, my babies, my children, sons and daughters."

Jesus Gets Violent

Tonight, September 23, 1992, as I am reminded of the two times when Jesus became physically violent when He threw the money changers out of the temple.

The first was when He ran the moneychangers out of the temple and the second when He took moneychanger and the people who endorsed what they were doing by conducting business with them and were thrown out of the temple.

If God's anger was inflamed against those who abused His "house of prayer" which was made with stones by the hand of man, how much greater will be His anger against those who destroy babies who are His living temples made by His hand, in His image, and in whom the Holy Spirit dwells?"

It seems that Jesus is sending a clear message to us today. Those of us who know Him and support the abortionist will likewise be thrown out of the temple of Christ's eternal resting place.

"He who is a partner with a thief hates his own soul. He hears cursing and says (does) nothing about it" Proverbs 29:24.

The Scriptures teach us that in God's eyes anyone who does nothing about abortion will be in serious danger of eternal judgment.

"If you do not deliver them that are drawn to death and those that are ready to be slain; if you say, behold we knew it not; does not he that ponders the heart consider it? Doth not he know it? And shall not he render to every man according to his works?" Proverbs 24:11,12.

Numbers, chapter thirty, tells us that silence brings a person into participation and agreement with the vow (commitment/action). Thus, binding them to either the blessings or consequences of the fulfillment of that commitment or deed done.

The Blood Of "Righteous Abel"

The Scriptures say that when Abel was killed by his brother, Abel's blood cried out to God from the ground.

Since God put such a heavy curse on one man who killed one family member, how great is the curse which awaits those by whom 30 million innocent babies were murdered?

Even the land was cursed because of Cain; "it bore no fruit". How great of a curse must there await a nation who commends the taking the life of innocent, defenseless little children.

> "...*And He (the Lord) said, What have you done? The voice of thy brother's blood crieth unto me from the ground. And now thou art cursed with a curse...*" Genesis 4:8-11.

Since God heard the cry of the blood of one innocent murder vicim how loud must be the cry of the blood of 30 million innocent babies who were killed in their mother's womb?

> "*And they cried with a loud voice, saying, How long, O Lord, holy and true, doest thou not judge and avenge our blood on them that dwell on the earth...*" Revelation 6:10.

Abortion is not only a contemporary issue. It has been a curse upon the land of several nations throughout the centuries of human existence.

The early church strengthened by the truth of the gospel addressed this issue through men of God such as Clemens of Rome who said:

> "...*the Scriptural laws were more humane to animals than were the Hellenes to human beings for they cast out their children as rubbish.*"

Tertullian also addressed this issue in a simple but wise manner when he said,

"What will be human is human."

It's A Baby

To determine whether abortion at any stage of the pregnancy is the taking of human life one needs ask only two questions. The first is whether that which is in the womb is human? The second is whether it is living? If the answer to both is yes then the abortion is the taking of human life.

Once the life of the unborn and defenseless has been devalued, who will be next? The aged? The infirm? The handicapped? The less intelligent? The less productive? Who sets the standards to determine who is worthy of life? Who plays God?

God is asking us to defend His children as we want Him to defend ours. In all this, Gods love and mercy is extended to forgive and heal. The heart of the law is mercy.

20

Candidate Criteria

In addition to evaluating whether the candidate would be an effective public servant it is needful to determine whether that candidate supports the biblical standards of morals and ethics.

In his second epistle to Timothy Paul enumerates the qualifications to be a pastor (Bishop). It is quite fascinating to see how they can apply to government office as well as the office of the Pastor (Bishop).

"This is a true saying. If a man desire the office of a bishop he desireth a good work" I Timothy 3:1.

Doesn't this apply to governmental service? After all, the Pastor and government officials are both in positions of service to God and man. The Pastor serves the spiritual needs of the people and the government official serves the social and legal needs of the people.

"A Bishop must be blameless" I Timothy 3:2a.

To be blameless is to have a consistently high moral standard of ethics in practice and faith. This doesn't mean they are sinless. Only that their path of life is consistently righteous in the same manner that the Gospel refers to Zecharias and his wife Elizabeth as "righteous." Luke 1:6

One may ask, what if a person holding an unacceptable position reversed it. Could they then be considered acceptable? Only if this change of opinion has had the time to develop into positive action verifying the authenticity of the change.

"The husband of one wife" I Timothy 3:2b.

A man or woman who will fulfill their commitments and oaths to their marriage will likely fulfill their oaths to public office. These fulfilled commitments establish a moral character of commitment, sacrificial loving and giving, honesty and integrity. Imagine if all of our governmental officials exemplified these characteristics.

This same principle applies to the single person. The underlying question being: Does that candidate fulfill their commitments and responsibilities? Are they reliable? Are they trustworthy?

"... vigilant..." I Timothy 3:2c.

He who is vigilant understands that the duration of the commitment and its' intensity is to be extensive. Anything good must be maintained in that "good" condition otherwise degeneration will set in which leads to destruction.

In his epistle, Peter offers us the Holy Spirit inspired admonition.

"Be sober, be vigilant, because your enemy the devil goes about as a roaring lion seeking whom he desires" I Peter 5:8.

The New Testament records that Judas Iscariot suffered from this problem and it led to his death and condemnation. The gospels record that Judas was the treasurer who stole from the purse regularly. He was covetous and a thief.

The devil had worked on his fallen nature which provided the open door for Satan to possess him. Satan was taking his time preparing Judas for the death blow which would betray Christ.

At the last supper the Scriptures attest to Judas becoming possessed by Satan then betraying Christ. Finally, after getting him to commit the abominable crime of betrayal, the devil condemned Judas who then committed suicide. All because he wasn't diligent to watch the state of his soul and relationship with Christ all the while examining his heart to see if there be any wicked thing in it.

Judas made the mistake of believing that no one could see his thievery. The fact of the matter was that God not only saw it but he was going to be exposed to the whole world through the Scriptures. Had Judas simply realized the omniscience of God he might has saved his soul.

One day I was speaking to a friend about the various experiences that a Christian has in their walk of faith. She asked me what is my greatest strength. I responded that it is knowing that at any time I can fall and sin. Therefore, because of this knowledge I know that I need to always be vigilant to guard the "doors" to my soul, which are the five senses.

I must beware of the thoughts I accept to dwell upon. I need to beware of what I allow my eyes to see, my mind to think, my ears to hear, my hands to do etc. In essence, I need to consciously and continuously heed the instruction of the Scriptures which says:

> *"Finally,brethren,whatsoeverthingsare*
> *true...honest...just...pure...lovely...of good*
> *report; if there be any virtue, and if there be any praise,*
> *think on these things"* Phillipians 4:8.

This admonition can be strongly applied in the lives of everyone and makes for a strong and productive candidate for office. This attitude will protect the candidate from doing anything improper and it will increase the effectiveness of their campaign.

Having people around the candidate who carry this belief will likewise make for a strong team of morally sound advisors. Consequently the advice given will be morally sound.

There are people who are not Christian but their life reflects the moral standards of Christianity. Does this mean that they are saved? Not at all. Salvation comes through faith in Jesus Christ and not through works. However, the point is that when addressing the political arena, we Christians need to remember that we are not electing our pastor, we are electing government officials who will establish their policies and decisions on the Judeo-Christian ethic.

"...Sober..." I Timothy 3:2d.

Sobriety infers that the candidate not be deluded by frivolity and distractions of the power, honor, attention, respect and influence of the office. All of their actions and policies are thought through to the end as to which would be best for the people he serves or will serve.

For those candidates who are running for office the first time this can be seen in the way they conduct their business and personal life. Are they honorable in their business dealings? Do they make light of serious issues? Do they give honor to those to whom it is due?

"...of good behavior, given to hospitality..." I Timothy 3:2e.

The candidate needs to demonstrate an openness and concern for those whose care is entrusted to him. They always consider the results of their actions upon those he or she represents. They treat everyone with respect and honor.

"...Apt to teach..." I Timothy 3:2g.

This person would have the ability to discern the truth, by clear thinking and effectively communicate it to his colleagues and constituents to gain further support for his policies.

Most mistakes made in life are a result of not having completely thought through the issue and taken into consideration all of the facts regarding the issue at hand. Can the candidate communicate their ideas and positions without being misunderstood?

Ronald Reagan was a excellent communicator. He was so effective that the national media gave him the title of "Great Communicator." This undoubtedly helped him get his legislative agenda implemented and foreign leaders were clear on his foreign policy.

In 1990 there was failure to effectively communicate to Sadam Hussein that the United States would not tolerate an Iraqi invasion of Kuwait. Consequently we fought the Gulf War.

"Not given to wine (heavy drinkers...)" I Timothy 3:3a.

Wine, in this context is referred to in a literal manner as well as a metaphor. In both, the element is that which distorts good judgment.

This person routinely does not allow himself to be overwhelmed by those things that can distort good judgment. For example, the desire for goods, services or money can have the same effect as intoxicating wine (alcohol).

I remember when working as a Purchasing Director I was negotiating with different companies. One of the salesmen I was negotiating with invited me to a lobster dinner. What is interestingly odd is that lobster is my favorite food and he had no way of knowing it. I felt that such an invitation was improper and sent the wrong message so I graciously declined the invitation.

The Book of Proverbs expounds on this:

> *"It is not for kings, O Lemuel, it is*
> *not for kings to drink wine: nor for*
> *princes strong drink: Lest they drink,*
> *and forget the law, and pervert the*
> *judgment of any of the afflicted.*
> *Give strong drink unto him that is*
> *ready to perish, and wine unto those*
> *that be of heavy hearts"* Proverbs 31:4-6.

"...No striker (troublemaker)..." I Timothy 3:3b.

This is a man of patience seeking to bring unity under the banner of what is best for the constituency. Who continually focuses on the truth and bringing people to it as embodied in the policies and decisions made. This person avoids stirring up trouble for selfish gains. The only time he is provoked is in defense of the truth and protection of the innocent.

This can be seen in President Bush's response to Iraq's invasion of Kuwait. He methodically, set the stage for Kuwait's liberation. He did not react spontaneously but rather he set his objectives and thoughtfully carried them out. Resulting in the largest and most diverse coalition of countries in the history of the world.

First U.S. troops were sent to Saudi Arabia to set a trip wire against further invasion by Iraq. The international coalition was formed. Israel was convinced to stay out of the conflict so as to not break up the Arab participation. The U.N. condemned Iraqi actions and leveled sanctions against it. Then at the appropriate time full military power was unleashed to liberate the country.

"...Not greedy of filthy money:..." I Timothy 3:3c.

It should be noted that this does not preclude the desire to better one's standard of living but rather addresses the extremes by defining the type of desire as "greedy" and the lucre he calls "filthy."

Let us recall that Paul's letter to Timothy said that it is the LOVE of money that is the root of all evil (II Timothy 6:10). Money itself is given to enjoy (II Timothy 6:17).

"... but patient, not a brawler, not covetous..." I Timothy 3:3d.

These attributes are possessed of a mature person who is not given to the impulses of the fallen nature but is content with what he has. Covetousness breeds jealousy which breed animosity in the hearts of those who have what is coveted and this will ultimately distort righteous judgment.
"One that ruleth well his own house, having his children in subjection with all gravity" I Timothy 3:4.

Obviously, not every political office holder is married with children and not every Bishop was married with children. The important point I believe to be made is that when a candidate's house i.e. his personal relationships with people, family and friends, business associates, etc., is honorable the possibility for success in governmental affairs increases. This is because they have been able to communicate, teach, exert authority and chastisement from a positive motivation achieving positive results.

"For if a man know not how to rule his own house, how shall he take care of the church of God?" I Timothy 3:5.

No matter what a person says they will do, in reality their future behavior will be consistent with what they have done previously.

What is concerning me is that our government is a large corporation, a business if you will. Unfortunately many office holders today do not have the basic knowledge of company and fiscal management from which to base their judgments and evaluations to make government most effective and cost efficient.

That's one of the reasons we have a multi trillion dollar debt. It is because most politicians cannot or will not comprehend the definition of "national debt" and its harm to the economy.

"Not a novice, lest being lifted up with pride he fall into the condemnation of the devil" I Timothy 3:6a.

It can be said that those most qualified to run the government and those most qualified to administer the affairs of the Church should have the qualification previously been successful in administering authority over people and/or family.

This Scripture admonition has a two fold protection designed in it. The first is the protection of the individual himself and second the protection of the assets and authority put into the trust of the individual in office.

A novice is one who has little or no experience in the "field" of endeavor. Therefore their skills in administering the responsibilities and authority of power will not be sophisticated and as effective as one who is skilled and experienced.

Giving authority to a novice could easily cause them to get caught up in the euphoria of the position and honor, losing the focus of their primary responsibility.

"Moreover he must have a good report of them which are without; lest he fall into reproach and the snare of the devil" I Timothy 3:6b.

Finally, the person considered for spiritual authority must have the respect of those in his community. The reputation of the candidate reflects who they really are. Likewise, any candidate for government office would need to have this same respect for several reasons.

First, to negotiate effectively whether it be with foreign leaders or those of opposing positions. Therefore the probability for success will be higher.

Secondly, negotiating with honor will reflect on the image of America worldwide and set an example for leaders and the American people.

During his years as President Ronald Reagan was known as a committed conservative. He was ideologically committed to certain principles and would not waver from them. One of his greatest attributes was that he was credible. He was a man of his word. When the Air Controllers staged their strike he threatened to fire them if they did not go back to work. They refused and they were fired.

The word in Washington was that even the opposition leadership respected him because whether you agreed with him or not you knew where he stood and could rely on his word.

Respect is the intangible asset that invariably assists any successful leader whether in Church, business or government.

A good name is important to have. Once you lose it, you can never get it back. Growing up, my parents continually admonished us to protect it. It may be that they read the Book of Proverbs which says that:

"A good name is rather to be chosen than great riches, and loving favor rather than silver and gold" Proverbs 22:1.

The Biblical standards discussed above in reference to I Timothy 3:1-6 can hopefully be seen to apply to non Christian candidates as well as those who share our faith.

From a political perspective the important point is that the candidate be committed to the moral principles consistent with the Judeo-Christian ethic.

A biblical case in point was Cyrus King of Persia of whom the Lord affectionately said:

> *"That (the Lord) saith of Cyrus, He is my shepherd, and shall perform all my pleasure: even saying to Jerusalem. Thou shalt be built; and to the temple, Thy foundation shall be laid"* Isaiah 44:28.

Picking a Candidate

When determining the individual person best suited for a particular position or office the most important factor to take into account is that of his past moral conduct, work experience success, and (if they are running for re-election) consistency of political position.

A good place to start looking for this information is with the various voter groups that track the positions of the candidates. The political party that they represent and the opposing parties as well. This way you can disseminate both views. You might be able to talk to the candidate yourself. Go to the political meetings and debates where they will be and listen to what they say and the rebuttles. You'd be surprised what can come out in a debate or town hall meeting. If the candidate is running for re-election then their voting record will be open to view.

Morality

First, their past moral behavior is the foundation of their future moral behavior. This will impact such things as their political, economic and social positions on future votes and issues. In the same manner it will determine the likelihood of that candidate's truthfulness and candor in addressing issues from the perspective of what is good for the country.

Remember, immorality is always a selfish behavior and looks only for immediate gratification of lusts and desires. It shuns commitment and will think or say anything that will satisfy those lusts.

A good definition of a politician is one who makes their decisions based upon the current poling data rather than on what is right for the constituents and the nation long term.

A statesman, on the other hand is that person who makes their decisions and positions based upon what is good for the people on an enduring basis.

Immoral character will always leave in question that person's faithfulness to their oaths. Trustworthiness will always be subject to the whims of self gratification on a temporal basis.

Jesus draws focus to this as recorded in Matthew 7:15 in warning his people about the false prophets:

> *"Beware of false prophets, which come to
> you in sheep's clothing, but inwardly they
> are ravening wolves. Ye shall know them by
> their fruits."*

It is reasonable to believe that this same caveat can be applied to government leaders as we evaluate the choices we are to make among those seeking our support. In doing so we can have a clearer picture of those prone to moral compromise and those prone to integrity

As Christians become more politically active their detractors accuse them of trying to legislate morality. The reality of the truth tells us that every law on the books today is an attempt to legislate morality. That's why there are laws against murder, fraud, rape, assault and battery to name a few.

The Christian position simply applies the common sense of adhering to those standards which have proven successful. Namely, the Judeo-Christian ethic.

The Dilemma

The next question to arise is, which candidate should be supported if none of them exemplifies the character qualities that have been addressed?

Needless to say, in today's political environment we find this to be the case in many races today. It would be great if all the candidates would exemplify the ideal character. However, what I do is to determine the background status of the candidates (regardless of the political party). I use the aforementioned Scripture of I Timothy 3:1-6 as my primary "voter's guide." Then I try to determine which candidate most closely aligns with those criterion.

One might ask if there are any issues that should have predominance in determining who to support. I most definitely believe so. The first issue is that the candidate chosen needs to be pro life. Remember, over one and a half million children are being murdered each year. These are God's children. Now ask yourself. If your children were at a baby sitter's house and someone broke in and began systematically torturing and killing them one by one, what issue would you want that baby sitter to be totally concerned? Paying her light bill? Cleaning the yard? Paying her taxes? Or saving your children from tortuous death?

The second most important issue is likewise a moral one. That of homosexual rights. If a candidate espouses to support the gay lifestyle they support the demise of the entire nation which is tantamount to treason and moral subversion. What then should a person do?

In the last Mayoral race in Los Angeles I was faced with an interesting dilemma. One candidate was extremely liberal in his political philosophy while the other was considered to be a moderate to liberal. On abortion, they were both pro-choice but the "moderate candidate" had a genuine disdain for abortion and believed it should not be funded with taxpayer money. Regarding homosexuality, the liberal candidate was outwardly pro-homosexual. The "moderate" liberal was accepting of them but did not believe that they should have special treatment.

On about every other point I found myself aligning with the "Moderate candidate." However, I had real problems with his stand on abortion. Therefore, knowing how serious abortion is to God I could not support either candidate.

One morning before the election the Lord gave me insight. If I did not vote for the "moderate" then that would add weight to the votes of the liberal. Therefore, I was voting whether I was casting a ballot or not. Therefore, I voted for the moderate. He won the election.

In conclusion, to determine the best candidate to support, I first of all suggest that serious and fervent prayer be offered to the Lord for His wisdom and knowledge to be granted to you. Second, do your homework and learn about the background and policy positions of the candidate. Are they morally qualified? Do they have the skills to govern? What groups or individuals are supporting that person. Third, if both candidates are pro abortion and for morally offensive positions, I personally would not work for either of them but I would vote for the lessor of the two "evils." If both are morally acceptable (e.g. pro-life, against homosexual rights and accept the Judeo-Christian concept of good government) then their skills and qualification background will need to be evaluated on the next tier of issues such as welfare reform, taxes, foreign policy, and other issues of prominence during the campaign.

For a person to assume authority without having an expertise to govern with mercy, truth, and justice can damage those governed in the same way as a physician not knowing how to use medicine can injure the patient.

Ability To Govern

John Chrysostom gives the analogy of a government official and a physician. Both are ministering to the needs of their patient.

He continues to say that a ruler (government office holder) has for instruments, his voice, anger, executioners, banishments, honors, gifts and praises; for medicines he has the law... his patients are those who are governed by him; the place to practice his medicine is in the courts of justice as well as the varied offices of government.

All these instruments of social health and protection of the body politic will profit nothing if he does not have the skill to use them properly. Rulers have a higher responsibility than physicians because they minister to the soul and the body while a physician ministers to the body only. Thus, it behooves us to be attentive of the choice we make in selecting the "physician" to minister to our nation.

Consequently, we can understand that Chrysostom would endorse the principle of Christians in government. After all it is difficult enough for the believer to maintain the understanding of responsibility in government. Much more for the heathen.

The caveat for the believer is to evaluate the academic qualification of the candidate for office as Chrysostom so eloquently stated that simply because one has medicines in the cabinet does not make him a physician. Rather he who knows how to use medicines effectively is the true physician.

Progression of Rulership

There are four areas of responsibility in the world today:
1. The soul
2. Family
3. City
4. World

There is the distinct relationship between spiritual and governmental authority. The prerequisites for one is the same for the other. The person who will be most effective in either realm will first govern his own soul then he will be able to rule over the rest in progression.

> *"nether he that pursueth political rule*
> *nor he that pursueth spiritual will be*
> *able well to administer it unless they*
> *have first ruled themselves..."* John Chrysostom

We are seeing a building block of governance. Each establishing the qualifications of the next level of leadership. Therefore, if one cannot govern his own soul he will not be able to govern his family, city and the nation.

However, when one has governed his soul, he will have the ability to take those things he learned in the struggle to effectively apply them to his family. In that process he will take all the experiences of family governance and apply them to his rule over a city and finally the nation.

So we see that the progression of responsibility and the experiences and lessons learned in the process of each will be used in the rulership of the next level.

In conclusion, I believe that we can draw two primary standards of evaluation when considering who to support for public office:

1. The person contemplating whether to seek public office would be wise to examine themselves in each aspect of life's responsibility as mentioned in this chapter.

2. One's determination as to the person to support may be based on the "progression of responsibility."

God Cannot be Confined to the Four Walls of the Church

Many nations and people have tried to confine the worship of God to the four walls of a Church building. In reality the prosperity of a nation always has been determinant upon its submission or rebellion to the laws of Nature and Nature's God. The former Soviet Union tried to do this when they attempted to separate Church and State. The consequences were disastrous, and the "Evil Empire" ultimately collapsed. The Church was victorious.

Without moral absolutes there is a void which is filled with confusion and a focus on self gratification without taking into consideration the ultimate consequences of their decisions, policies and positions.

21

Christian Responsibilities and Accountability

Christian involvement and awareness in public affairs is critical to establishing and sustaining a healthy, safe, prosperous and secure society.

Edward Gibbon, noted historian and author of *"The Decline and Fall of the Roman Empire"* attributes the fall of the Western Roman Empire, in great part, to the fact that the clergy discouraged Christians from holding public office. He reasons that for several hundred years there were several attempts to invade the Western Roman Empire—all were unsuccessful. Therefore, what different circumstances were present that made the Empire vulnerable to successful invasions?

Gibbon contends that the primary differential was that Christians left positions of government service. Subsequently, these offices became occupied by corrupt and incompetent officials. Consequently, erosion in the moral fabric ensued and this deterioration provided the breach through which the invaders could successfully attack.

Other reasons which made the empire vulnerable were that too many non- producers were outnumbering those who were productive. Society was fragmented by languages (shall we consider English to be the official language?). The Church focused on the City of God at the expense of abrogating the Christians' responsibility to the City of Man. Bureaucracy had greatly expanded (gee, this sounds like the federal government today). The abuse of the welfare state overburdened society and drained the resources of the empire (are we sure this was the Roman Empire instead of 20th century America?). Politicians were getting rich without paying their fair share of taxes. Taking into consideration these elements of decay and we see an empire crumbling at its' foundation.

What's Expected?

Christians have a responsibility to attain the greatest productivity with the gifts God has given them in order to effect the greatest good for the individual and the nation. We can see this illustrated all through the Scriptures from the life of the Kings of Israel, to the story of the Roman Centurion whose love of God opened the door to the healing of his sick servant. However, there is one particular parable that Jesus taught which serves to teach the believer about their personal responsibility to be productive with the earthly talents that God has given.

The parable I am referring to is that of the "talents. (Matthew 25:14-30) One servant was given five, another was given two and the other was given one.

The servant who was given one talent knew what his master was like. Therefore, he should have known that to do nothing would anger his master and bring irrevocable retribution upon himself. What was the ultimate concern of the master? That the servant was lazy as demonstrated by him not even putting the talent to the money changers to make interest.

A second item of concern to the master was that the "lazy servant" relied upon his own understanding of the knowledge that he had. This servant feared that the master would be angry if he tried to do something with the talent and lost it. This fear was based on the knowledge that his master was a hard businessman. The servant's problem was that he knew the facts but made a lame excuse to cover up his laziness. This lead to his condemnation.

Contemporary Christians can learn from the errors of the lazy and fearful servant who did not use his "talent" wisely. If government institutions and other socio-political institutions are not accessed by the Body of Christ's believers to effect positive and healthy policies for the nation, then there will be a similar accounting.

The lazy servant feared, did nothing, and he was judged. It is clear that Christians who likewise are fearful of ridicule or failure and hide their talent regarding the public life of our nation will very likely suffer the same judgment.

The principle is the same. God has given us social and government institutions which direct public policy. To abrogate our civic responsibilities potentially puts the authority of these offices in the hands of others who may not hold to such moral positions as espoused by the Judeo-Christian ethic.

The master not only chided the servant, he called him "wicked" and "lazy." He showed no sympathy nor accepting of his excuses. Because of the servant's knowledge, the master held him to account for the talent that he possessed.

Reliance on one's ideas and perception without the mind of Christ can, as the lazy servant found out, be very dangerous.

Christians need to seek the mind of Christ concerning His positions and attitudes towards issues concerning life and faith. morals and conduct.

"There is a way which seems right to man, but the end thereof are the ways of death" Proverbs 14:12.

It well for us to remember that God does not have need for our opinions. Rather we need to seek His. After all, He is God, He is the One who gives us our life breath, He is the one who holds the universe together and He will sit on the judgment seat at that great day. Therefore, it is beneficial for us to put aside our personal opinions about political activism and civic responsibility and understand what God is saying to His people today.

The Christian body of believers has been given by the "Creator" a nation and government which provides for citizen government. Those citizens can direct the course of the nation. Either along the path of righteousness, life and prosperity or over the precipice of destruction.

Think of it, God provides a nation whose citizen government can change world history for the better, protect the lives of the unborn, implement sound fiscal, social, military and foreign policies as well as being a leader in establishing positive role models in government and society in the world for future generations.

Let's reflect on the rewards of the faithful and wise servants who put their talents to work. They were not only commended but they were rewarded with great abundance.

On the other hand if God showed such retribution against one lazy servant who was only given one talent to work with how great will be the retribution of the True Master of Heaven when He returns to the earth. What will it be like when He finds a nation which, due to the absence of the Christian influence, has found itself grown over with the "thorns" of disease caused by immorality, the chains of massive debt, the graves of the youth who were shot going to school?

The fruit of citizen involvement will be as jewels in the crown of salvation for those who take this responsibility seriously. For those who don't, it will be as wood, hay and stubble. We are given the opportunity to choose.

God expects us to exercise the gifts He has given us to bring positive results in all that we do as we acknowledge and honor Him in those endeavors.

Thus, the concluding message is that God is looking for fruitfulness in the use of our talents that He gave us regardless of what they are or how many we have. Secondly, God judges us based upon what has been given to us and not on the gifts, ability or productivity that others possess. What may seem to be insignificant to us is of great importance to God. Keep in mind that all gifts from God come from the same throne and the same Holy Spirit.

It is very important to take note that the consequences of the slothful servant's non-productivity was physical and spiritual. He first lost his "talent." Then he lost his soul.

> *"Take therefore the talent from him, and give*
> *it unto him which hath ten talents...*
> *And cast ye the unprofitable servant into outer*
> *darkness; there shall be weeping and gnashing of teeth."*

Christians have been given the "five talents" of Christ's presence, wisdom, understanding, counsel and power. Likewise Christians have been given the "two talents" of human ability and wealth. Finally, we are given the "one talent" of the favor of God: Glorify Christ Jesus through them and thus release the peace and blessing of God upon the land.

The Judgment

To emphasize the fact that the gifts and judgment of God are natural and supernatural, Jesus immediately follows the parable of the "talents" by speaking of the final judgment. The judgment that Jesus hands down is based upon works done in this life (Matthew 25:31-46).

The blessing for those who fulfilled these works and the judgment for those who did not do those works were likewise eternal. One unto joy and the other unto damnation.

One might ask: But that sounds like we are saved or condemned by our works. Doesn't the Scripture say that we are saved through faith?(Ephesians 2:8).

Our works testify and manifest our faith. All acts of kindness are selfless and all the inaction taken when we saw a need were acts of selfishness.

Recall, if you will, the parable of the rich man and Lazarus (Luke 16:20-25). The rich man was so burdened by his wealth he neglected the needs of Lazarus. When they both died their roles were reversed and it was the rich man who suffered.

James admonishes the Christians to not simply express good wishes to those in need but requires us to apply our works to our faith. Thus, the reality of our faith will become rooted in the life and works of the believer bearing forth the reality of the believer's faith.

"If a brother or sister be naked, and destitute of daily food,
And one of you say unto them, Depart in peace, be ye warmed
and filled; notwithstanding ye give them not those things which are
needful to the body; what doth it profit?" James 2:15,16.

Jesus reinforces this principle in the story of the widow and the two mites. (Mark 12:42,43) This woman came into the temple while Jesus and the disciples were there. They were watching the wealthy men put in their donations of gold and jewels and then this widow woman puts in her meager offering.

Jesus says that she gave more than anyone. She, out of her love gave all she had. Therefore, we see that Jesus is not so interested in the amount of work or contribution that we offer to Him but rather what is our attitude and how the gifts offered relate to our ability.

So it is in the political arena. God is expecting us to use whatever abilities and gifts we have been granted to effect positive change and moral truths in government. To some He will call to run for office to others simply to write letters or answer telephones for political candidates. Everyone is asked to do something.

How do these Scriptures relate and apply to Christian involvement in politics? First, every man, woman and child has been given a talent or talents from God. By using these talents in the political arena the greater good for the nation and mankind would be accomplished.

Biblical precepts, principles, judgments and ordinances directly affect the life and survival of a nation. As a father extends his love and appreciation to those who assert themselves to help and protect his children from danger, the Lord takes the same view with believers who put their gift(s) to use in the service of the Lord to lead mankind toward the light of His righteousness.

Those who assert themselves to protect and lead a nation to live in accord with the truths of Christ bring them into fellowship with the Father who is in heaven bringing His blessing of peace, health, prosperity and joy.

Those who actively participate in the nation's system of government for these purposes are giving of themselves to serve others. Thus, in a real way we begin to fulfill the commandment of the Lord to "...*love thy neighbor*...".

22

Russia Yesterday, America Tomorrow

Before the fall of the Soviet Union I had dramatic experiences which led me to go there. Through the many experiences I had before and after to this trip it was made very clear to me how the sovereign hand of God reigns in the kingdoms of man.

I have included the testimony of my experience in this book. I trust it will be enjoyable and interesting as you join me on this journey.

Visions and Dreams

I was living in Cedar Rapids, Iowa when the 1980's began. In the fall of 1981, I began having dreams about going to the

Soviet Union via airplane coupled with the conviction to go there.

The idea of going to the Soviet Union was always repugnant to me. In fact, I always told the Lord that there were two things I would never do. First, go behind the Iron Curtain and secondly, live in California (I'm presently living in Los Angeles).

The dreams kept recurring. Once I dreamed of flying in a fighter bomber. As I crossed the Soviet border I saw thousands of icons inlaid with pure and dazzling diamonds all around the edge.

Having been raised in the Orthodox Church I understood that these icons represented Christians behind the Iron Curtain. According to Orthodox teaching, mankind is the "Icon" of Christ since we are made in God's image (icon).

Another time I dreamed that I was instantaneously taken to the South Pole, where I froze. Then I was quickly brought back to my bedroom. The message became clearer and I consented to go to the Soviet Union.

The Invitation

Shortly thereafter my cousin called from Wichita, Kansas and said, "Tony, there's a great offer through the University to go on a trip." I asked, "where to?" He responded, "The Soviet Union." Hearing that I wanted to say "thanks but no thanks." Thinking I could postpone the inevitable I told him I would let him know later. What made this all the more dramatic was that he knew nothing of my dreams concerning the Soviet Union.

Obedience or Rebellion

After a couple weeks he called to see if I was going on the trip. I literally opened my mouth to say "no" when the Holy Spirit said to me "you're going!" With great reluctance I agreed to go.

Angelic Visitation

That evening I became very concerned and I felt that if God wanted me to go to the Soviet Union He was going to want me to be a witness for the gospel. With the chill of diplomatic relations between Reagan and Brezhnev, and the Soviet hostility toward religion, I would get into trouble.

In feeling the need for wise counsel I called a man who had walked with the Lord for decades to see if he had any insight. When I shared with him my dilemma he told me told me that he sensed the presence of the Lord..."I believe you are supposed to go."

When I hung up the telephone I looked up and saw a warrior angel standing over six feet tall in the doorway. He held a large flaming sword. He spoke without moving his lips. He said "fear not for I shall be with you." During the trip we had one particular experience which I believe evidenced the angel's presence. I will speak of this later.

Prophetic Word

A few days later I recall being in our family kitchen and telling them of the news that I was going to the Soviet Union. Suddenly my brother turned to me and began to prophecy that I would be used by God to deliver the answer to someone's prayer.

New York...An Unexpected Visit

In order to make connections for my flight to Moscow I had to stay overnight in New York. On the day of departure, at 1:10 p.m. I went downstairs to catch the limousine from my hotel to the airport (the limousine was set to leave in just fifteen minutes).

As I walked outside to get into the limousine Jesus said for me to go into the restaurant and order lunch. I struggled with His instructions (typical of the fallen nature of man) because I didn't think there would be enough time. However, I wanted to be obedient to the Lord so I went into the restaurant anyway.

When the waitress came to take my order Jesus said for me to tell her about Him. When I did she responded in a way I did not expect. Smiling broadly she said "Oh yes, I'm a Russian Jew and I like hearing about that," She went on to tell me that her grandfather fought in the Russian revolution as a "White Russian."

After our conversation was finished, the Lord told me to leave for the airport (I never did order lunch). I did, getting into the limousine on time.

Upon arriving at the airport I found that our plane was late. In trying to occupy our time we visited with our tour guides to get some insight about attitudes and views of the Soviet people and government about Americans and their own internal affairs.

As a matter of conversation I brought up the name of Father Demitri Dudko. They quickly responded by saying "...you don't even mention his name...he is 'hot' on the government list." I thought to myself, *"what a great way to start a trip to the Soviet Union."*

Red Square at Midnight...The Amazing Prophecy

We arrived in Moscow at mid evening. We were held up in Customs for over four hours. What we didn't realize was that Reagan had banned the sale of some technical equipment to the Soviet Union and we were feeling some of the repercussions. I thought to myself, *"what another great way to start a trip?"*

Finally we arrived at the hotel Russia which was across from the Kremlin and Red Square. The bed in my room was little more than a cot. Couple that with the time difference, I found myself lying down and wide awake. At midnight I still could not sleep so I went to Red Square. As I stood in the center with St. Basil's Cathedral on my left and the Kremlin in front of me I asked God, *"Lord, I've been obedient in coming to the Soviet Union. Please tell me, why did you send me here?"*

The Lord replied, *"I am about to destroy the Soviet Union."*

I immediately thought of Ezekiel chapters 38 &39.

The Lord responded again to my thoughts, *"I AM not refer-ring to that. I AM going to pour out my Spirit in such a way that the whole Communist system will collapse."*

Upon hearing this prophecy I began to pray and implement the weapons of spiritual warfare in Red Square. Praying that God would send His Spirit to destroy the Communist system.

As I prayed, the Lord spoke to me again and said, *"The 'So-viet Union and Eastern Block nations will soon become one of the greatest centers of evangelism the world has ever known."*

Hearing this, I began to pray for the peoples of the Soviet Union and Eastern Block nations to receive the infilling of the Holy Spirit with His enabling power and strength.

The Lord's Warning...

On one of our tours we visited an Orthodox church which was turned into a museum. There I saw the vessels used in the Orthodox liturgical worship now put on display as "relics of antiquity."

Upon looking at those items the Lord said to me, *"Just one hundred years ago, if someone would have said that Holy Russia would be antichrist they would have been laughed out of the country. If it hap-pened here it can happen in America. Be warned."*

Communists Preaching the Gospel?

On another day we visited the Kremlin. While there we went into the Orthodox Cathedral. Inside the Cathedral, the walls were covered with icons depicting biblical events and persons.

Upon leaving the Cathedral the Lord stopped me at the door and said to turn around and make the "sign of the cross." When I did one of the custodians at the entrance table gently smiled at me.

When I walked outside the Lord said something that astounded and puzzled me. He said, *"The Communists are preaching the gospel and they do not even know it."*

I pondered the question: How a government which professed atheism, was preaching the gospel? I then asked the Lord how this could be?

He began His explanation by posing a question, "What are icons?"

Immediately the Orthodox theology concerning icons came to mind. Namely, that icons are not just pictures, they are "writings." Icons are given that name because they present the written Bible in picture form. It is helpful to remember that the Early Church did not have "xerox" copies of the Scriptures and many people were illiterate. Additionally, the intent of the Byzantine icon in its use of physical features, is to draw the attention of the viewer to the spiritual quality of the person or scene depicted rather than the physical quality.

Remembering this brought to mind that in Byzantine iconography any saint depicted needed to be pictured in the context of the event describing why they were "sainted." For example, Mary will never be pictured without Jesus. The reason being that without Jesus she loses her identity.

Then the Lord explained, "The Communists hold the Russian Orthodox iconography in high reverence for, what they call, "their artistic value." Thus they take pride in showing off their Orthodox Churches and the icons they possess."

As I pondered upon this He brought to mind the following Scriptures:

"Some indeed preach Christ even of envy and strife and some also of good will: The one preach Christ of contention not sincerely, supposing to add affliction to my bonds: But the other of love, knowing that I am set for the defense of the gospel. What then? not withstanding, every way, whether in pretense, or in truth, Christ is preached; and I therein do rejoice, yea and will rejoice" Philippians 2:15-18.

"For the wisdom of this world is foolishness with God. For it is written, He taketh the wise in their own craftiness" I Corinthians 3:19.

"He disappointed the devices of the crafty, so that their hands cannot perform anything. He takes the wise in their own craftiness: and the counsel of the shrewd is carried headlong" Job 5:12,13.

"My word shall not return to me void but it shall accomplish that which I have purposed it to do" Isaiah 55:11.

Then it all came together. The Communists displayed the iconography and architecture of the Orthodox Churches as a testimony of Russian culture to generate revenues from tourism. In so doing the millions of people who annually were shown such "works of art" were presented the gospel of Jesus Christ in picture form. Thus, the Communists were presenting the gospel of Jesus Christ to all those who entered the Churches and because He promises to bring fruit from his word, those who hear it will be blessed.

From Moscow to Kiev

On the way from Moscow to Kiev, a private conversation took place with our tour guide. Her name was Tammarah and she represented herself as a member of the Soviet Intelligencia. She proudly and confidently proclaimed the "gospel of communism." I felt impressed by the Lord not to say much but rather just listen to her. After our arrival I was to find out why.

The first night in Kiev I received a telephone call from the same tourist guide. She invited me to meet her in the coffee shop to talk about communism. I responded to her invitation by agreeing to talk about communism if we can also talk about Jesus. She agreed.

When we met she shared about her beliefs in communism. I shared my beliefs in the capitalist system and then our conversation gradually focused on my testimony of Jesus Christ.

After a few minutes she "confessed" that she had a grandmother who was a devoted Christian with whom she had been very close until her passing a few years previous.

I then shared with her that before I came on this trip I had received a prophesy that I would be the instrument God was going to use to answer a prayer for someone. I then shared that the Lord wanted her to know that her grandmother was alive, living in heaven and she was praying for her. Upon hearing this she began to weep. Then she related to me how her grandmother raised her in the faith of Jesus and at the age of eight she was baptized.

Monastery of the Caves

While in Kiev we went to a place called the Monastery of the Caves. This is an Orthodox Monastery that was literally built down into a mountain. The reason being that as the monastery grew in numbers they had no money to buy land so they dug deep into the mountain to accommodate the growing numbers of monastics.

We were taken down into the mountain where we saw the bodies of some of the monks which had been dead for over one thousand years. The miraculous was that some of the bodies were perfectly preserved and we were able to see them, clothed with the vestments of worship while others had decayed.

Though the color of the skin was dark, the features of the person were clearly seen. As I looked upon the person's body I saw that the skin in the wrist was broken and a honey-like substance could be seen.

We were later told that when the bodies were discovered, some had actually given off a perfume-like fragrance. Having seen and heard all this caused me to remember the Scriptures telling about a dead man being thrown into the tomb of Elisha. When the body touched Elisha's bones the man who was thrown into the tomb came back to life. The power of God was still indwelling the "temple of God." (II Kings 13:21)

Upon leaving the monastery my cousin asked our tour guide what attributed to such preservation? The tour guide said the scientists were working on the answer to the question but they feel that the atmospheric conditions were so perfect that the bodies became preserved.

My cousin responded, *"If that's the case then why were some bodies preserved and others right next to them were not?"*

The tour guide paused and then said, *"I'm an atheist, but if you believe in God then the righteous were preserved and the wicked were not."*

Here we see the official atheist government of the Soviet Union presenting to us the miraculous sign of God's power. What an antithesis to Communist atheism. However, I see it as God's way of demonstrating that He reigns in the governments of man. Here He is using "dead" men to confound the "wisdom" of atheism.

Leningrad (St. Petersburg)

After a few days in Kiev we went to Leningrad now known as St. Petersburg. We were taken to Orthodox churches that were turned into museums, as well as other sights of interest.

On the last day of our visit to Leningrad (St. Petersburg) it was the close of the day and finishing our tour. My cousins and I realized that we needed to buy gifts for our relatives. We decided to leave the tour to go to the "tourist shop."

Time got by us and when we left to go to the hotel it was rush hour. Imagine being in a city of nearly three million people about 98% of whom use the Metro subway system to go to and from work. A sea of people filled the streets.

We were on the way to the subway (Metro) when my cousin said "Tony, there is a Metro station across the street. Why don't we go there instead of going up the street to the one where you were told to go?"

I said "okay."

When we entered the station, the people were so numerous we could not see the floor. We stepped off to the side to get our bearings. From that view point it was like watching a river of people flowing down the escalator to the Metro.

It so happened that there were two Soviet flight attendants standing off to the corner as if to be waiting for us. I vividly remember seeing their flying wings pinned to their uniforms.

We asked if they spoke English and one replied, in her Russian accent, "a leetle." When we asked her which subway to take to the hotel, she said "We are going that way follow us."

Oddly enough we saw several levels from which to approach the Metro. We needed to take the Metro on the second level, and I was going to take the Metro on the first level. Thank God for the flight attendants. If we hadn't met them I wouldn't want to imagine where we might have ended up.

Upon arrival to the hotel we noticed that the flight attendants began going back towards downtown. My cousin asked, "didn't they say that they were going to the hotel?" My other cousin and I said "yes." Then the reply came, "then why are they going back towards downtown?"

We all thought it was odd and yet interesting. If they were angels their actions spoke to us that they were going the way to the hotel for our sakes. After all, they only said that they were going that "way." They did not say that they were actually going to the hotel. Were they angels? I don't know for sure but there are some interesting points to consider.

1. Had we gone to the Metro station I originally planned on we would have missed them.

2. Soviets who speak English are very rare. In addition, neither of us spoke any Russian.

3. The directions I was originally given to get back to the hotel were incomplete and if we had not encountered the flight attendants we would have taken the wrong subway. No telling where we would have ended up.

4. We needed help.

5. We ended up at the hotel without incident.

The Return Home

Upon our arrival back to New York City we gathered our baggage and promptly sought a taxi to the hotel. Getting into the taxi we noticed the driver speaking "broken" English with a strong European accent. We asked him where he was from. He said: "The Ukraine." He went on to share that he had just arrived in the United States.

In a city of thousands and thousands of taxi cabs I can't believe that meeting this man was mere coincidence. Think of it, the last person with whom I spoke before I left for the Soviet Union was of Russian heritage and the first person I spoke with upon my return was of Ukrainian descent. Both countries being members of the former Soviet Union.

After arriving back in Cedar Rapids, Iowa I shared with friends and relatives the prophetic word that God gave me. The responses were varied. Some accepted it. Some were puzzled and some, I'm sure, thought I had a great imagination.

The Young Russian Woman

In 1994, after moving to Los Angeles, California, I was at a church service where I met a young Russian woman. Wanting to encourage her I shared my experience in Russia. After the church service was over she came to express a word of encouragement to me.

She said that for thirteen years after accepting the Lord she tried to leave the Soviet Union but was prevented by the government. Then, the same year I went to the Soviet Union and for some unknown reason the government decided to change their mind and let her go.

Deliverance for the Soviet Union...Warning for America

Shortly after the fall of the Soviet Union the Lord spoke these words to me, *"I view a nation as a person. For example, Israel is the name of man Jacob, yet it refers to the whole nation of people. The Soviet Union having been one "person" has just experienced an exorcism of the spirit of the Anti-Christ. Now that same spirit is looking for another "host body." It has found one in America who has rejected Me and my statutes of life."*

The Church is the spirit and conscience of America. Will she rise up and expel the evil which has begun to possess her "body and soul" or neglect her moral responsibilities?

The Soviet Union collapsed in the same manner as the Lord prophesied to me. What is interesting is that it happened through the prayers and actions of people. It did not come with a bolt of lightning from heaven. It came through the hand of people as they were moved by their heart's hunger for freedom, and the Spirit of God which opened the "door" for their deliverance. Much the same way that God opened the Red Sea for the Hebrews to leave Egypt—He parted the water and they walked through.

When the Berlin wall came down it was hammered and chiseled by people who wanted to be free. It was God's favor and power combined with their labor and effort which brought down the wall of bondage. We can surely see that God reigns in the kingdoms of man through the hearts, mind, and hand of men and women who are obedient to God because of their love for Him.

Conclusion

Shortly after the Communists took power in Russia in the beginning of the twentieth century, a socialist intellectual addressed a meeting of five thousand people. They were all "invited" to hear of the great virtues of Socialism and Communism.

After several hours expounding his thesis, the speaker concluded his remarks. He was confident that he presented an irrefutable dissertation. Then, in an intimidating manner he opened the floor to anyone who had a comment.

Slowly a priest arose from his seat and went to the podium. In a smug and condescending manner the speaker said to the priest that he only had five minutes. The priest replied that he would not even need that much time.

The priest stepped up to the microphone and said that he had just one thing to say. Repeating the Church's Easter morning proclamation he said, *"Christ is risen."*

Upon hearing this, all five thousand attendees thundered their response, *"Indeed He is risen!!!"*

During the era of the cold War the Church was the first line of defense against Communism. For example, in 1954 there was a meeting that attracted hundreds of thousands of people. Although it was intended to be non-political, it quickly turned into a rally against Communism.

Even though the Russian and Eastern European peoples endured great persecution and trials, they kept their faith and ultimately they were free. While there was little those people could do politically, great men like President Ronald Reagan were unrelenting in their efforts to destroy the "evil empire." The work of the free world and the prayers of the saints brought freedom.

Science and Religion

The acceptance of the philosophy of secular humanism by many in public office and leadership has led down the path of disenfranchisement from godly principles. However, in the latter part of the twentieth century science has discovered what the Bible had been teaching for thousands of years.

One such notable example is the discovery that laughter is medicinal. King Solomon wrote this in the Book of Proverbs 17:22:

"A merry heart is like a medicine."

Medical science has recently discovered that babies can hear while they are in their mother's womb. Interestingly, the Book of Luke taught this when it recorded the account when Mary went to see her cousin, Elizabeth while they were both pregnant. Elizabeth told her,

*"And whence is this to me that the mother of
my Lord should come to me? For, lo, as soon*

*as the voice of thy salutation sounded in mine
ears, the babe leaped in my womb for joy"* Luke 1:43,44.

Centuries ago Christopher Columbus proved what the Bible had always been saying: The world was round.

"It is He that sitteth upon the circle of the earth,..." Isaiah 40:22

Moral High Ground

The Church has always possessed the moral high ground in any debate. Unfortunately some in the Church slept while injustices were done.

For years Christians responded to the abortion issue in three ways: Activist, passive, and "I don't care." (I was one of the passive ones, until I saw a picture of an aborted baby.) Fortunately, greater knowledge has helped draw and focus Christians into active involvement.

Many positive results are occurring. The tide of public opinion is changing, medical science is endorsing the pro life position that abortion is the taking of a human life. This can be seen in that three of the last four Presidential elections have been won by the Republicans who endorsed a Human Life amendment in the Party platform.

Recent Success

In recent years we have seen great success in restoring the civil rights of Christians. In Smyrna, Georgia, a young girl sought to use the Community center to teach dance and share her faith in Jesus. She then received an ultimatum forbidding prayer in the facility. After appealing to the American Center For Law and Justice her rights were honored.

In the early 1960's the United States Supreme Court struck down prayer in the schools. However, in recent years an organization called the National Coalition On Bible Curriculum In Public Schools was formed. This organization set out to reintroduce the teaching of the Bible in public schools, and they have been successful. One lady's action is bringing the Bible back into the classroom.

One of the great accomplishments of Christian involvement in civic affairs is the 1994 landslide victory which gave control of the Congress to fiscal and social conservatives. The tide of activism by Christians in government and the political process is accelerating.

There is a long way to go in restoring America back to the sound foundation based upon the Judeo-Christian Ethic. Unfortunately, we have seen the United States Supreme Court give an endorsement of homosexuality when it struck down Colorado's Amendment Two. It also struck down a parental notification law regarding minors seeking abortion.

Love, Commitment and Intelligence

As Christian involvement in the political process continues we can expect to see greater resistance by those who hold contrary views. Some are sincere and others will be diabolical in their efforts to block any success.

It is of great importance that the proponents of the Judeo Christian philosophy, standards and principles expound their positions with intellectual honesty, sincerity and objective truth. Likewise, love must be the response we give to those who are disagreeable, or even hostile to our faith, morals and political positions. However, love as defined in the Christian context, can be defined as asserting the positions and truths of the Judeo Christian ethic but without malice, pride and prejudice to those who hold a contrarian position. We need remember that Jesus died and conquered death for them as well as for us.

As I mentioned earlier in this book, the fourth century Emperor Diocletian seriously persecuted Christians. However, it did not succeed in crushing the faith. The faith grew greater and greater. In fact more and more Christians became bold in proclaiming their faith. This helped dispel the misconception that Christians were disloyal and hated humanity.

The reason that Christianity spread was because the central message of the gospel was God's love for humanity and His desire for people to love one another. This appealed to so many in the Empire who felt unwanted and unloved.

The Dual Purpose of Christians in Politics

As we set forth our efforts to bring sound moral values to public policy, we need to be cognizant of the gospel's dual nature affecting our spiritual and earthly lives.

When our efforts in this life reflect the light of Christ in both kingdoms more people will be attracted to the radiant Christ and the godly principles and morals He established by which we are to live.

Therefore, with intelligence and wisdom, let us persevere to bring sound moral values to public policy. Likewise let us continue reflecting the light of Christ's love. Let us respect those with whom we disagree, all the while holding strong to our convictions.

We have souls in need of salvation, and a nation in need of God's principles for "...*life, liberty and the pursuit of happiness...*"

Bibliography

Title	Author
Eastern Christendom Published by N.Y. Putnam c1961	Nicholas Zernov
America's Dates With Destiny Published by Thomas Nelson Publish- ers 1986	Pat Robertson
Newspaper 1-12-96	Daily News
Politically Incorrect Published by Word Publishing 1994	Ralph E. Reed, Jr.
Time Magazine	1-15-96
New World Order Word Publishing	Pat Robertson
Standing Firm Harper Collins Publishers Zondervan 1994	Dan Quayle
Homilies on Matthew's Gospel	John Chrysostam
Homilies on 1 Timothy	John Chyrsostam
Homilies on Romans 13	John Chrysostam
Los Angeles Times 1-15-96	
The Discourses Published by Paulist Press 1980	St. Symeon The New Theologian
The Plan Thomas Nelson Publishers, c1989	Pat Robertson

Philokalia   Church Fathers
Published by Faber and Faber Ltd.

History of Christianity   Erdmans
Lion Publishing 1977

New Millenium   Pat Robertson
Word Publishing

City of God   St. Augustine

Jesus Called Her Mother   Dee Jepsen
Bethany House Publishers 1992

Christian Coalition Report 11-8-94

Mythe of Seperation   Bartlett

Life of St. George   Fr. Constantine Nasr

Social Triumph of Ancient Church   Shirley Jackson Case
Harper and Brothers 1933

Christian Church in the Cold War   Owen Chadwick
New Look at the Church State Problem
Allen Lane 1992

Kingdoms In Conflict   Charles Colson with
Zondervan Publishing House c1987   Ellen Santilli Vaugh

Re-Civilizing America   Law and Justice Feb. 1994
Re-Evaluating Religion in Pub. Life   Law and Justice Mar. 1994

Early Church and the World, Early   Cecil John Cadoux
Christian Church
Edinburgh, T&T Clark 1925

Los Angeles Times 2-22-96

Christian American-March 1994

The Teachings of the Church Fathers
Herder 1966

John R. Willis

Movieguide Report to the Industry

Christian Film and Tele-
vision Commission

Los Angeles Times-February 22, 1996

Daily News-April 2, 1996

The Spirituality of the Christian East
Cistercian Publications 1986

Tomas Sidlik

Jerome, 6th Novella

Postmodernism: Undermining America's
Moral Conscience

700 Club Fact Sheet

Journey Through the Divine Liturgy
Theosis Publishing Co. 1991

Archpriest Constantine
Nasr

Letter to the Magnesians

Ignatius of Antioch

Time Magazine-January, 12 1996

Don Nardo

Reader's Digest-January 12, 1996

The Roman Empire
Lucent Books 1994

Edward Gibbon

The Decline and Fall of the Roman
Empire
Viking Press 1952

Athanasius of Egypt

Orville J. Nave A.M.,
D.D., L.L.D.

On the Incarnation of the Word

Naves Topical Bible
Riverside Book and Bible House
Iowa Falls, Iowa

James Strong, S.T.D.,
L.L.D.

Strong's Exhaustive Concordance of the
Bible

Unity of the Church

Dr. Antoine Mansur

To order additional copies of

Jesus, Politics and the Church

please send $19.99* plus $3.50 shipping and handling to:

Tony Nassif
PO Box 2754
Toluca Lake, CA 91610-0754
213-878-6532

*Quantity discounts avaiable.